access to

The EASTERN *and* CENTRAL EUROPEAN STATES *1945 – 1992*

John Laver

ughton

ADLINE GROUP

Acknowledgements

The publishers would like to thank the following for permission to reproduce material in this book: Popperfoto, p. 56 and David King Collection, pp. 23, 83, and 84.

Every effort has been made to trace and acknowledge copyright. The publishers will be happy to make suitable arrangements with any copyright holder whom it has not been possible to contact.

Orders: please contact Bookpoint Ltd, 39 Milton Park, Abingdon, Oxon OX14 4TD. Telephone: (44) 01235 400414, Fax: (44) 01235 400454. Lines are open from 9.00 - 6.00, Monday to Saturday, with a 24 hour message answering service. Email address: orders@bookpoint.co.uk

British Library Cataloguing in Publication Data

A catalogue for this title is available from the British Library

ISBN 0 340 69780 6

First published 1999

| Impression number | 10 | 9 | 8 | 7 | 6 | 5 | 4 | 3 | 2 | 1 | |
| Year | | 2005 | 2004 | 2003 | 2002 | 2001 | 2000 | 1999 |

Cover illustration provided by Sygma Ltd.

Illustrations by Ian Foulis & Associates Ltd, Plymouth
Typeset by Sempringham publishing services, Bedford
Printed in Great Britain for Hodder & Stoughton Educational,
a division of Hodder Headline Plc, 338 Euston Road, London NW1 3BH
by Redwood Books, Trowbridge, Wiltshire.

Contents

Preface

To the general reader

Although the *Access to History* series has been designed with the needs of students studying the subject at higher examination levels very much in mind, it also has a great deal to offer the general reader. The main body of the text (i.e. ignoring the 'Study Guides' at the ends of chapters) forms a readable and yet stimulating survey of a coherent topic as studied by historians. However, each author's aim has not merely been to provide a clear explanation of what happened in the past (to interest and inform): it has also been assumed that most readers wish to be stimulated into thinking further about the topic and to form opinions of their own about the significance of the events that are described and discussed (to be challenged). Thus, although no prior knowledge of the topic is expected on the reader's part, she or he is treated as an intelligent and thinking person throughout. The author tends to share ideas and possibilities with the reader, rather than passing on numbers of so-called 'historical truths'.

To the student reader

There are many ways in which the series can be used by students studying history at a higher level. It will, therefore, be worthwhile thinking about your own study strategy before you start your work on this book. Obviously, your strategy will vary depending on the aim you have in mind, and the time for study that is available to you.

If, for example, you want to acquire a general overview of the topic in the shortest possible time, the following approach will probably be the most effective:

1. Read Chapter 1 and think about its contents.
2. Read the 'Working On ...' sections at the end of Chapter 2 and decide whether it is necessary for you to read this chapter.
3. If it is, read the chapter, stopping at each heading to note down the main points that have been made.
4. Repeat stage 2 (and stage 3 where appropriate) for all the other chapters.

If, however, your aim is to gain a thorough grasp of the topic, taking however much time is necessary to do so, you may benefit from carrying out the same procedure with each chapter, as follows:

1. Read the chapter as fast as you can, and preferably at one sitting.
2. Study the summary diagram at the end of the chapter, ensuring that you understand the general 'shape' of what you have just read.
3. Read the 'Working On ...' sections (and the 'Answering essay

questions' section, if there is one) and decide what further work you need to do on the chapter. In particularly important sections of the book, this will involve reading the chapter a second time and stopping at each heading to think about (and to write a summary of) what you have just read.

4. Attempt the 'Source-based questions' section. It will sometimes be sufficient to think through your answers, but additional understanding will often be gained by forcing yourself to write them down.

When you have finished the main chapters of the book, study the 'Further Reading' section and decide what additional reading (if any) you will do on the topic.

This book has been designed to help make your studies both enjoyable and successful. If you can think of ways in which this could have been done more effectively, please write to tell me. In the meantime, I hope that you will gain greatly from your study of History.

Keith Randell

1 Introduction: Eastern and Central Europe, 1945-92

POINTS TO CONSIDER

This chapter will introduce you to some of the main events and themes of this period in the history of Eastern and Central Europe. It will give you a broad idea of how and why Communist regimes were established in the region, how those regimes then developed, and how and why they were overthrown in the late 1980s. Your aim in first reading this chapter should be to understand the broad sweep of events throughout the region before considering particular developments in more detail.

KEY DATES

1945	End of the Second World War
1945-8	Establishment of Communist regimes in Poland, Czechoslovakia, Hungary, Romania, Bulgaria and East Germany
1953	Death of Stalin
1956	Hungarian Rising
1968	Invasion of Czechoslovakia
1989	Overthrow of Communist regimes in the region

1 Eastern and Central Europe

> **KEY ISSUE** What was the geographical and historical context of this region prior to the period of this book?

'Eastern and Central Europe' in this book will be used to define those countries which occupied the area between the liberal democracies of Western Europe and the Soviet Union and which were under Communist rule between the late 1940s and late 1980s. They were Poland, Czechoslovakia, Hungary, East Germany, Bulgaria and Romania. Since these states were within the Soviet sphere of influence, the region was also referred to frequently as the Eastern Bloc or the Soviet Bloc. Yugoslavia and Albania, although also Communist, are not included in this book since they followed largely separate paths of development.

Geographically, Eastern Europe comprised the great Northern European Plain (included within much of Poland and East Germany) between the Baltic Sea and the Carpathian Mountains; the Carpathian Mountains themselves; the Danube Plain; and the edge of the Balkan peninsula to the South and East (including Bulgaria and Romania).

Eastern Europe after the Second World War

Politically, the region had developed national identities and modern institutions more slowly than Western Europe. For centuries it had been part of the great multinational empires of Hapsburg Austria, Russia and Turkey. Nationalist movements developed in the nineteenth century, but rarely achieved independence. Economic development was also slow. The region did not experience the urbanisation or industrialisation of countries like Britain and Germany, except in a few areas like Bohemia and Moravia. However, pressures were created by growing populations and the desire of peasants for land reform in societies still largely dominated by a semi-feudal aristocracy. The countries varied in size: at the end of the 1980s Poland was the largest, with a population of 38 million. Romania had 23 million, the GDR 16 million, Czechoslovakia about 12 million, Hungary 10.5 million and Bulgaria 8.5 million.

The First World War had a significant impact upon Eastern and Central Europe. Before 1914, conflicts within the region had arisen mainly from competition between the Great Powers for influence. However, by 1918, 'self-determination', the right of national groups to decide their own futures, had become one of the war aims of the victorious Allies. The collapse of the Austrian and Russian Empires opened the way for the creation of new states. Poland achieved its independence for the first time since its partition at the end of the eighteenth century. Czechoslovakia and Yugoslavia were completely new states. Hungary achieved full independence, although it was treated as a defeated power. Bulgaria and Romania were already independent states, but that independence was confirmed after the War.

2 Between the Wars, 1918-39

> **KEY ISSUE** What were the main political developments in the region between the two World Wars?

The euphoria of new nationhood was short-lived. The states of Eastern Europe faced many problems. Could they retain their independence? That independence had been achieved because of the defeat of the Russian, German and Austrian Empires. Should Germany and the new Soviet Union recover their strength and ambition, the future of smaller states sandwiched between them would be uncertain.

There were other more immediate political problems. Despite the principle of self-determination built into the peace treaties of 1918-19, most of the Eastern European states contained national minorities, for example Turks in Bulgaria, Hungarians in Romania and Germans in Czechoslovakia. These minorities had few effective guarantees. Also, the region had no tradition of democracy, and only Czechoslovakia was to retain democratic government almost until the Second World War. Elsewhere authoritarian right-wing regimes assumed power. Although these regimes were not as extreme as the Nazi or Soviet varieties, their dominance retarded economic and social progress. Some of the countryside in Eastern Europe was made up of large estates, although many had been redistributed to the peasantry after 1918, except in Hungary. Peasants were mostly subsistence farmers. Population growth, which was twice the European rate as a whole, added to economic pressures made worse by the depression of the 1930s.

The governments of these smaller states were of course aware of the threat from expansionist Germany and Italy. Poland, Czechoslovakia, Romania and Yugoslavia sought refuge in alliances with France, but the Czechs and the Poles found the promises of support hollow when Hitler expanded German power eastwards in 1938 and 1939. Hungary took a different route, allying itself with Germany.

3 The Second World War, 1939-45

> **KEY ISSUE** What was the experience of the Central and Eastern European states during the Second World War?

The fates of the Eastern European states varied during the Second World War. Czechoslovakia had already been broken up and occupied beforehand. In 1939 Poland was divided between Germany and the USSR, and suffered terribly: 17 per cent of its population died during the War. Hungary, Bulgaria and Romania were allies of Hitler when he invaded Russia in 1941, but as the Soviets turned the tide and rolled the Germans back from 1943 onwards, these states came under direct threat from the advancing Red Army. By 1945 the USSR controlled most of the region. This was largely to determine the fate of Eastern and Central Europe for the next 40 years.

4 The Establishment of Communist Control, 1945-48

> **KEY ISSUE** How and why was Communism established in the region in the years immediately after the Second World War?

Britain and the United States recognised the key role of the Soviets in defeating Germany. Churchill tried to negotiate a reasonable deal for Poland, but the British and Americans soon came to accept that Eastern Europe was now within the Soviet sphere of influence. However, nobody was quite sure of Stalin's intentions. It was generally accepted that, at the very least, he was determined to have friendly governments on Russia's Western borders, as a buffer against any future attacks on the Soviet Union. However, as mutual suspicion between the Soviets and the West developed in what became known as the Cold War, anti-Communist commentators assumed more sinister intentions. It was believed that Stalin aimed to extend Soviet power as far into Western Europe as he could. It was also assumed that Stalin had been intent from the start on imposing Soviet-controlled Communist governments in Eastern Europe.

The reality was more complex. Before 1947 Stalin acted cautiously, often making political concessions. For example, he carried out his promise to Britain not to support Communist insurrection in Greece. Stalin was determined to destroy the power of pro-German élites in the occupied countries, and this was achieved by political and economic measures shortly after the War. However, it was not a simple case of the Red Army forcibly imposing Communist rule on unwilling populations. Many people recalled that the Communists had campaigned for radical reform before the War, and a mood for change now prevailed throughout Europe. People also recognised that the Communists had an honourable wartime record of resistance against the Germans after 1941. There was no wish to restore the old regimes. Consequently in Eastern Europe there was considerable popular support for, as well as opposition to, the Communists.

New political arrangements had to be made. The process was complicated because several countries in the region had governments-in-exile operating from their wartime bases in Britain. They could not simply be restored to sole power: these governments no longer commanded automatic support in their homelands, and nor were they all acceptable to the Soviets.

As the Cold War intensified, Stalin imposed more control on Eastern Europe, and more discipline on Communist Parties. This control was imposed gradually. After the War there were coalition governments in the Eastern European states. These states were often known as 'People's Democracies', and their governments were coalitions of Communists, Socialists, members of Agrarian parties, and various democrats. These groups had certain common aims, among them the eradication of the legacy of fascism and major land reform. However, the Communists were in a strong position because they usually occupied the most important ministries, including those for Propaganda and the Interior (which controlled the local administration and the security services). Other political parties were then gradually eased out by the Communists, whilst the Socialists were often forced to unite with the Communists. Leading democratic politicians went abroad or were arrested. Non-Communists sometimes paved the way for their own destruction. For example, the Communist 'coup' in Czechoslovakia in 1948 was successful as much due to weakness and division amongst non-Communists as to deviousness and naked ambition on the part of the Communists themselves.

5 Stalinist Europe, 1948-53

> **KEY ISSUE** What was the nature of Stalinist Europe?

After 1949 Stalinist influences became more pronounced. Links between native Communist Parties and the Soviet Party were strengthened. Purges involved the sacking, imprisonment or execution of Communist Party members on a large scale. These practices had been typical of the USSR in the 1930s, as Stalin had reinforced his dictatorship. Stalinist-type purges now became commonplace in Eastern Europe, and were directed first against non-Communists, then against individuals and factions within the Communist Parties themselves.

As significant in the long term as these political developments was the institution of Stalinist-type command economies. These were based on the 1930s Soviet model of centralised planning and direction of resources, with priority given to the development of heavy industry and capital goods, and the collectivisation of agriculture. There were rare exceptions: attempts to collectivise Polish agriculture were abandoned after 1956.

Communism demanded conformism and sacrifice. But the changes to people's lives were not all negative. The old élites in Eastern Europe lost their privileges. Long-delayed development of national resources got under way. There were social advances, particularly in literacy and education. Expectations were raised, and there were sometime rises in living standards, albeit at the price of living under authoritarian regimes buttressed by censorship and the state security services.

As in the USSR in the 1930s, the Stalinist economic model proved quite effective in raising output in states with a primitive economic base. It was less effective in more advanced economies like Czechoslovakia and East Germany. Economies were no longer peasant-based. But the rate of economic growth began to decrease significantly. This was often not evident in official economic statistics, which were doctored to present an optimistic picture. Although some growth continued it was clear to Communist regimes by the 1960s that economic reforms were necessary. Most states produced some variations on the Soviet model, usually incorporating attempts at increasing initiative and making economies more responsive to supply and demand economics rather than the priorities of central planners. But the effects of reforms were limited, and there was a reluctance to relax central planning mechanisms too far.

In Hungary in 1956 and Czechoslovakia in 1968 reformers from both inside and outside the Communist Party tried to implement major changes: economic reforms, allowing for more individual initiative, and political reforms which would have challenged the Communist monopoly of power. The Soviet response was to invade both countries and replace the regimes. This suggested that although some limited economic reform might be tolerated, Moscow would allow nothing too radical. Abandoning state controls would have unacceptable political implications. There was an additional problem in that the economies of Eastern Europe and the USSR had been made deliberately interdependent, making changes in one area potentially disruptive throughout the region.

Political dissent was harshly treated in what were essentially one-party states. There were factional struggles among the Communists themselves, but they tended to go on behind the scenes. Dissent could not be tolerated since it threatened the 'leading role' of the Communist Parties, and also brought the threat of Soviet intervention.

6 Destalinisation and Soviet Intervention, the 1960s and 1970s

> **KEY ISSUE** How and why did the Soviet Union intervene in Hungary, Czechoslovakia and Poland?

Stalin died in 1953. He had ensured that loyal Communists were in control of Eastern European regimes. But Khrushchev, his successor, attacked his memory in 1956, criticising Stalin's purges and ruthless methods of rule. Khrushchev launched a policy of destalinisation or relaxation of the most arbitrary and rigid aspects of Stalinism, without compromising the power of the Party. This policy caused confusion in Eastern Europe. Khrushchev suggested that other states introduce reforms, but the Stalinist leaders were unwilling. However, when popular pressure from outside the Hungarian Communist Party threatened Communist control in 1956, the USSR physically crushed the Hungarian Rising.

In 1968 Soviet tanks were again in action, to crush a reform movement in Prague. This time the pressure for change had been coming as much from within the local Communist Party as from outside. Even so, the Soviets were not prepared to tolerate a threat to what was still in essence a Stalinist political and economic system.

In the 1970s and 1980s there were crises of a different nature in Poland. Here the reform movement was dominated by a mass organisation, *Solidarity*. The Polish regime was forced to try to suppress the movement in order to avoid Soviet intervention.

7 Reform and Collapse in the 1980s

> **KEY ISSUE** How and why were the Communist regimes transformed in the late 1980s?

Popular pressure for change in Eastern Europe developed during the 1980s. Failing economies undermined the tacit social compact whereby people had tolerated Communist single-party rule in return for the promise of rising living standards. Increasing contacts between countries, more travel, the spread of influence of the media - all part of the world becoming a 'global village' - meant that ordinary people were becoming more aware than ever of the differences in quality of life between Eastern and Western Europe. The regimes found it increasingly difficult to control the media. Even intellectuals who had previously supported the regimes were siding with the discontented working class.

The key factor was the attitude of the Soviet Union. In 1985 Mikhail Gorbachev came to power there and introduced his own reform programme of *glasnost* ('openness') and *perestroika* ('restructuring'), in an attempt to breathe life into the ailing Soviet economy. Although Gorbachev intended that the Communist Party would retain control of the reforming process, once the Party began to relax controls it became difficult to manage reform. Economic reform prompted political change. As the Stalinist system in the USSR was painfully dismantled, the Soviets no longer had the will or power to dictate policy to their former client states in Eastern Europe. Indeed, Gorbachev positively encouraged reforms there, cutting the ground from beneath his fellow Communist leaders.

Popular pressure for change continued to grow, and in the late 1980s all the regimes caved in relatively easily, with the exception of Romania. There was a debate within the governing élites of the Eastern European states about how to respond to pressure. The 'traditionalists' wanted to tread carefully, whereas the more radical reformers wanted to completely dismantle the old political system and introduce free market economies.

The collapse of Communism was rapid, partly because events fed off each other. The starting point was Poland. Here the regime tried to reach an accommodation with a long-established opposition. It failed, with the result that the Communist Party effectively collapsed and reconstituted itself as a Social Democratic Party.

In Hungary the Communists allowed competitive elections in 1990. The Communists received less than 9 per cent of the vote and conceded power to a non-Communist Government.

Change in East Germany was sparked by an exodus of its citizens to the West via Hungary, which opened its borders with Austria. Although the long-serving East German leader Honecker resigned in the face of popular resistance in October 1989, demonstrations continued and the Berlin Wall was breached in November. A reform-minded Communist became Prime Minister, but in March 1990 the former Communists were heavily defeated in elections by the Christian Democratic Union.

In Czechoslovakia there were also public demonstrations in

November 1989, undeterred by police attacks. The Government resigned in December to be replaced by a largely non-Communist Government with Václav Havel, a former playwright and dissident, as President.

In Bulgaria the ruling Communist Party transformed itself into a Socialist Party following mass demonstrations in November 1989. The new Party won a majority in subsequent elections, but it had to form a coalition Government and was then forced into opposition by the end of 1991.

Romania followed a very different pattern. There the dictatorial rule of Ceauşescu seemed secure as late as November 1989. But following public demonstrations Ceauşescu fled the capital, was captured and killed. Thousands died in the subsequent street fighting. The Communists continued to exert considerable influence in the succeeding Government set up after multi-party elections.

With the exception of Romania, the political transition from Communism to post-Communism was remarkably smooth in Eastern and Central Europe. This was partly due to the statesmanship of Gorbachev; partly due to the fact that many Communists jumped on to the reformist bandwagon; above all, it was due to the general recognition even by hard-liners that the regimes, which had never enjoyed much legitimacy with the ordinary people despite all the propaganda, had simply lost all credibility. They had lost it through their inability to sustain economic growth with accompanying benefits, which had they continued might have been some compensation for people lacking a genuine political voice. Failing economies meant that the 'social compact' between rulers and ruled was broken; and improved communications, which made the peoples of Eastern Europe more aware of better conditions in the West, only added to the resulting disillusionment with Communism.

8 Problems in the Post-Communist World, the 1990s

> **KEY ISSUE** What problems faced the post-Communist regimes as they entered the 1990s?

The euphoria of political change did not last long. As the Eastern European states entered the 1990s and the post-Communist era, major problems faced new Governments ill-equipped to deal with them. Firstly, could democracy sustain itself in countries which had little or no tradition of it? What would be the role of presidents and parliaments? How would parliamentary democracy develop when political parties lacked clear identities or mass memberships, and frequently split into factions? Secondly, the economic transition from Communism was far less smooth than the political transition. How would unstable Governments cope with economic change? There was a general expectation of moves towards some kind of market economy. But there was no precedent for a socialist economy transforming itself into a capitalist one. Governments had no easy answer to phenomena such as inflation, rising prices and unemployment, which accompanied the dismantling of the cumbersome state-run economic systems of the Socialist era. It was soon obvious that there were no easy solutions.

9 Basic Issues in Eastern Europe, 1945-1992

> **KEY ISSUES** What were the most important issues affecting the countries of Central and Eastern Europe in the period 1945-1992?

In order to come to a broad understanding of the period covered by this book, it is useful to address certain key questions. Always we should be aware both of common trends and the differences between individual states as they dealt with the political, economic and social issues of almost half a century. The following are key questions:

a) How was it that the Communists came to power in the years immediately following the Second World War? How significant was the wartime experience of these countries? Did Communists come to power purely through the power and pressure of the Soviet Union, or were there popular pressures for change at work in Eastern Europe which assisted the growth of Communism? How did the Communists, who were but one of several political forces on the scene, manipulate themselves into complete power and establish one-party states?

b) How did political and economic systems develop in the Communist states? How influential was the Soviet Stalinist model? What was the role of the Communist Party in these states? How successful were these regimes in promoting economic and social progress, and in particular adapting to difficulties and changing circumstances? Was the failure to sustain economic growth the principal reason for the ultimate collapse of these regimes? How did the Communist states relate to each other and their Soviet patron? How significant were organisations like the Warsaw Pact and COMECON?

c) Change was rapid at the end of the 1980s. Disillusionment and popular protest against the regimes grew. Why did the regimes collapse? Was the Soviet refusal to bale out the Communist regimes of Eastern Europe the key factor? To what extent did events in one state influence events in the others? Why, with the exception of Romania, were the revolutions relatively bloodless?

The issues outlined above gave their shape to the period from 1945 to the early 1990s in Eastern and Central Europe and will form the themes of this book. The more recent the issues, the more tentative are likely to be the conclusions, since we do not have much historical perspective when considering the evidence. Nevertheless, it is important that we examine the evidence with a critical eye, in order to try to assess the significance of this recent period in Eastern European history.

Making notes on 'Eastern Europe, 1945-92'

It is important to grasp the general issues and understand the basic Eastern European framework of events. To assist you, you may find the simple chronologies in some of the chapters helpful in giving you an idea of developments during this period. At this stage you will not recognise all the events listed, but a chronology will act as a useful frame of reference as you work through the chapters in the book, even though it lists only some of the main events. You may wish to construct your own chronology as you go along, although try to avoid becoming bogged down in too much detail.

Essay advice

In most of the chapters of this book there are essay titles and advice on how to tackle them. When considering an essay question at this level, it is a good idea to follow this procedure:

1. Consider the key words and phrases in the question.
2. Decide what is the main theme of your answer, and how you will approach it. It will help to draw up a brief plan. Remember that you are not only being asked to write down facts, or a narrative, of what happened, but also to construct an argument. Evidence should be used to back up your argument, whatever it is.
3. A short introductory paragraph may be used to establish the context of your intended argument.
4. Write the main body of the essay, using paragraphs as appropriate.
5. A concluding paragraph should be used to synthesise your theme, that is, pull together the main threads of the arguments that you have made in the main body of your essay, and also to emphasise key points. The conclusion should not be used to repeat your arguments at length, you should not contradict any earlier arguments you have made, and you should not use the conclusion to introduce new material at this stage.

At the conclusion of several chapters in this book there are examples of essays. At the conclusion of the final chapter there are typical questions which require knowledge and understanding of the whole region, or a substantial part of it. However, whatever the question, the advice given above holds good if you are to produce a relevant answer which addresses the issues.

2 The Communist Takeover, 1945-48

POINTS TO CONSIDER

This chapter will focus upon the period of the three years following the end of the Second World War in Europe, explaining how and why Communist regimes came to power in the countries of Central and Eastern Europe. As you read the chapter you should consider Stalin's strategy and the role of the USSR, in addition to the efforts of Communist Parties in the various states. You should develop some understanding of the tactics which these Parties used to get themselves into positions of influence, and the degree to which their success was due to popular support, clever manipulation, or Soviet influence in the background.

KEY DATES

1945 End of Second World War
Decision to form National Unity Government in Poland
Stalin supported Communist coup in Romania
Potsdam Agreement finalised territorial changes in Eastern Europe; Germany divided
1946 Bulgaria: Communists gained majority in parliamentary elections
Czechoslovakia: Communists gained parliamentary majority
Romania: National Democratic Front gained a majority
1947 Hungary: Communists increased membership in Government
Poland: Communists forced opponents out of office
1948 Czechoslovakia: Communist 'coup'

In the years immediately following the Second World War Communist regimes were established in each of the countries which are the focus of this book. To a large extent these regimes were established due to the influence of Stalin and the Red Army. The USSR wanted to ensure there were Communist regimes in an area vital to its own security. However indigenous Communist movements had some popular support, partly due to their wartime resistance to the Nazis.

1 The Communist Resurgence: From Occupation and Struggle to Liberation

KEY ISSUE To what extent did the Communist Parties of Central and Eastern Europe increase their strength and support by the end of the Second World War?

Communist parties in Eastern and Central Europe were in the fore-front of the underground struggle against Nazi control of the region between 1941 and 1945, once the USSR became involved in the War. As the tide of war turned against the Nazis from 1942, the Communists were in a potentially strong position, not so much through their own strength but because they could rely upon Soviet support in the background. Nevertheless, the situation in each country was complex: not only were Communists fighting against Nazism, they were also opposed to the right-wing regimes often in power in these countries before 1939. They also had to define their relationship with other left-wing parties and with Stalin, whose own long-term ambitions, strategy and tactics in Eastern and Central Europe were still not clear to many people at the time.

a) Poland

The situation of the Polish Communists was particularly complex. Poland's position was vulnerable, largely the product of its geography and history. Sandwiched between the great powers of Russia and Germany, and at one time the Austro-Hungarian Empire also, Poland had been swallowed up in the eighteenth century and regained its independence only after the First World War. Between the World Wars it experienced inflation, strikes, tensions between Poles and ethnic minorities, and fear of Nazi Germany and Stalinist Russia. In 1939 Poland was carved up between Hitler and Stalin. In the following War, Poland suffered more than six million dead, a figure proportionally higher than that of any other combatant nation.

Stalin distrusted the Polish Communist Party and had brutally dissolved it in 1941. He allowed the Party to be reconstituted in 1942 and encouraged it to form a Popular Front with other parties on the Left. This was a common tactic at this time because nowhere did the Communists command a majority of popular support. At the same time Stalin fostered a parallel Polish Communist leadership in Moscow, should the need arise for more direct intervention. To add to the complexity, there was a Polish Home Army and a non-Communist Polish Government-in-Exile in London.

In 1943 Wladslaw Gomulka, deputy leader of the Polish Communist Party, was ordered to negotiate with the Government-in-Exile. However, there were disagreements about where the Polish borders should be defined. Stalin sent Boleslaw Bierut to work with Gomulka. Bierut refused to make concessions to the Socialists and rejected Gomulka's attempts to form a Council of National Unity.

Stalin supported Bierut and decided to use military force to get his way in Poland. In February 1944 the Red Army began the liberation of Poland from Germany. Stalin's new Polish Committee for National Liberation, established in Lublin under Bierut and dominated by Moscow-based Communists, was to be the political instrument of

---

BIOGRAPHY: WLADSLAW GOMULKA (1905-82)

Gomulka was born in Galicia when it was part of Austria-Hungary. He worked as a locksmith and in an oil refinery, joining the Communist Party in 1926. An active trade unionist, he was frequently imprisoned for his Communist activities. Gomulka showed his independent spirit early on, ignoring Stalin's order to Polish Communists not to resist in 1939 and fighting the Germans instead. Hence Stalin's mistrust of him, which was to resurface later. After the War Gomulka became Deputy Prime Minister. However, criticism of Stalin led to his dismissal in 1948 for 'nationalist fervour', imprisonment (1951-6) and expulsion from the Party. He was readmitted after destalinisation in 1956. Between 1956 and 1970 Gomulka was Party leader, until forced to resign over riots against price rises. Gomulka was a strong advocate of a specifically Polish form of Socialism: one which allowed for private land ownership, toleration of the Church and a relaxation of police powers. Although this was popular inside Poland, Gomulka was also criticised for his strong commitment to the USSR.

BIOGRAPHY: BOLESLAW BIERUT (1892-1956)

Bierut was born near Lublin and joined the infant Polish Communist Party in 1920. He went to Moscow in 1938, returning to Poland in 1943 to organise the takeover of Poland by the Communists. Bierut remained a loyal, hardline Stalinist, and was responsible for the deposition of Gomulka after the War. Bierut was President of Poland between 1945 and 1952, and Prime Minister between 1952 and 1954.

---

control. However, as in other Eastern and Central European states, Stalin also wanted Socialist support: in Poland's case because the Communists were fighting a difficult civil war against the Polish Home Army, which looked to the London Poles for help.

In January 1945 Stalin formally recognised Bierut's Committee as the Provisional Government of Poland. In the same month the Polish Home Army was disbanded, its leaders invited to Moscow and imprisoned there. It was the beginning of a brutal undercover war between Communists and anti-Communists, following the end of the Nazi occupation.

Britain had a particular commitment to Poland, having gone to war in 1939 in its support. Therefore Britain and the USA would not recognise the new Government until Stalin at the Yalta Conference agreed to free elections and the inclusion in the Government of a broad range of representatives. Several groups did agree to support Bierut. But then Stalin appeared to have second thoughts about a broad coalition and stalled negotiations.

The Provisional Government of National Unity was finally formed in June 1945 and contained members of the Communist, Socialist,

Peasant and Catholic Parties. The Socialist Edward Osóbka was Prime Minister, and the Government was joined by Stanislaw Mikolajczyk, former leader of the Government-in-Exile. Stalin's tactic appeared to work, since the Allies recognised the new Government, and it implemented the Potsdam Agreement on Poland's frontiers: they were shifted westwards into former German territory to compensate for loss of Polish land in the East to the USSR. Poland more than any other country in the region was central to Soviet political and strategic thinking, and Stalin was creating a buffer between Soviet territory and possible invasion from the West.

b) Hungary

Communist fortunes in Hungary also benefited from a Soviet military presence. Before 1939 Hungary's small Communist Party had been illegal. In 1941 Hungary joined in the German attack on the USSR, stimulating resistance from left-wing groups. In 1942 the Hungarian Socialist Party joined forces with the Peasant Alliance. Hitler distrusted his ally, particularly as anti-Nazi feeling gained strength, and Germany occupied Hungary in 1944. The Socialist-Peasant alliance was suppressed. The Communists, led by László Rajk, allied with the Socialists, and the idea of a Popular Front took root, more strongly than in Poland.

The Red Army invaded Hungary in September 1944. Hungarian Communists continued to encourage the idea of a Popular Front 'from below', with themselves pulling the strings - a common tactic throughout Eastern Europe. A National Independence Front of several political groups was set up, but mainly influenced by the Communists. Stalin may well have seen no particular advantage in supporting revolution in Hungary: certainly the exiled Hungarian Communists who arrived with the Red Army were ordered to put a stop to revolutionary tactics. Stalin ordered the Communists to join a coalition government. He was anxious to keep control of change rather than allow the Hungarian Communists to come to power in their own independent way. Mátyás Rákosi was given the task of rebuilding the Party according to Moscow's instructions. The old Government was ousted at the end of 1944 and changes quickly followed. With the Red Army established in Hungary, Imre Nagy, the Communist Minister of Agriculture, announced the expropriation of large landholders in January 1945.

c) Czechoslovakia

Although Stalin pursued similarly cautious tactics in Czechoslovakia, there were distinct differences in the Czechoslovak experience from that of Hungary and Poland.

The uniting of the Czech and Slovak lands at the end of the First

World War was not an easy marriage, and nationalist sentiments were to affect even Communist politics. It was partly an economic issue: although the economy was relatively developed by Eastern European standards, about 80 per cent of Slovaks were poor peasants. Czechoslovakia was the only genuinely democratic state in the region between 1919 and 1939, and the Czech Communist Party, able to operate openly, regularly won over ten per cent of the vote in national elections, not just in the more industrialised Czech lands but also in the rural areas of Slovakia and Ruthenia. Therefore the Communists had the advantage of an established powerful base, unlike neighbouring states where Communist parties were small and illegal.

Czechoslovak politics suffered similar complications to those of Poland during the War. Like the Poles, the Czechs had a Government-in-Exile in London, run by President Eduard Beneš. At home, Klement Gottwald led Czech Communists against the Nazis. In Slovakia, partisans fought the pro-German Slovak Government. Meanwhile Stalin signed an agreement with Beneš' Government in 1943 promising to respect Czechoslovakia's prewar borders. In August 1944 a Slovak National Rising was organised from London, but it was the Communists who gained considerable influence in the multi-party Slovak National Council. As elsewhere, the power of the Red Army was the ultimate arbiter, and when it invaded Slovakia in October 1944 the Communists' future seemed secure. Although Stalin dealt with Beneš in London, a Czech Communist headquarters was also set up in Moscow. Consequently the Czech and Slovak Communists were well-equipped to play a full part in postwar politics once Stalin had decided upon his tactics.

d) Romania

Romania's Communists also benefited from Soviet military strength as the War approached its end. Prewar Romania contained Hungarian, German and Jewish minorities, not properly assimilated, and the country was economically and socially backward compared to its neighbours. It depended upon Germany economically and for protection against Hungary, yet in 1940 it was forced to cede Bessarabia and Northern Bukovina to the USSR, and Northern Transylvania to Hungary. Romania joined the German invasion of the USSR in 1941 and suffered once the tide turned against the Nazis. From 1943 Romanian Communists tried to persuade other left-wing parties to form an anti-Hitler coalition against the right-wing regime, although the Communists themselves suffered from internal divisions. Stalin imposed Gheorghe Gheorghiu-Dej on the Party in 1944, with orders to form a multi-party alliance. The Communists, Socialists, National Liberals and National Peasant Party formed the National Democratic Front in June 1944.

The Romanian Government switched to the Allied side, and the Communists and Socialists went their own way: whilst supporting the

War, they also campaigned for democracy and radical land reform. Their proposals to break up estates and cancel peasant debts won them peasant support.

As elsewhere, Stalin played something of a waiting game in Romania. The Red Army entered Bucharest in August 1944 and therefore could be used to impose his will if necessary. However, Stalin could afford to wait: in September he got Churchill's agreement for a dominant Soviet interest in Romania and so was content to let the Romanian Communists make their own bid for power. When a new Government was set up in December 1944 under Nicolae Radescu, it contained a Communist deputy. The Communists were strengthening their hold.

e) Bulgaria

Soviet military strength was also crucial in Bulgaria. Before the War Bulgaria had a right-wing Government. During the War this was opposed by Bulgarian Communists, whose partisan groups tied down the Bulgarian Army and received aid from Moscow. Although Bulgaria was never occupied by Germany, Stalin declared war on Bulgaria in September 1944. On the day of the invasion there was a Communist coup in Sofia. A Communist-dominated Fatherland Front Government was set up, which was to prove, as elsewhere, a vehicle for the Communists to gain control.

f) Assessment

Therefore as the Second World War came to an end in Poland, Hungary, Czechoslovakia, Romania and Bulgaria, the Communists were emerging from a period of struggle both against their own governments, and in some cases against Nazi occupation, to play a prominent role in the formation of new governments. Only in Czechoslovakia had the Communists been a substantial political force before the War. Therefore, although the Communists had won many plaudits for their resistance activities, the principal reason for their emergence on to the national stage was the support they had from the Red Army, which was in actual occupation or in the background in case the need for more overt action was deemed necessary. Much would depend on Stalin's attitude. He was primarily concerned with Soviet security and the need for friendly regimes along Soviet borders. However, he had made certain agreements with his Western allies. Also at this stage it was not certain that the wartime alliance would totally disintegrate, and Stalin preferred to allow the indigenous Communists, who in many cases had been nurtured in Moscow, to ally with other left-wing and even centrist groups to increase their influence before making a more overt bid for power.

2 1945-8: The Communist Advance

> **KEY ISSUE** How and why did Communist regimes come to be
> established throughout the region by 1948?

The three years from the end of the War saw the Communists establish
control in all the countries analysed above. A common Communist
ploy was termed in Hungary 'salami tactics': this meant Communists
allying with other parties before elections or after governments were
formed; then making alliances with different groups or unscrupulously
changing their stance so as to gradually sow disagreements amongst
other parties and whittle away opposition to themselves. Eventually
the Communists would be left in control. The process was virtually
complete with the Communist takeover in Czechoslovakia in 1948.

a) Poland

The unity of Communists and Socialists in Poland did not long survive
the War, despite their commitment to radical reform. Non-Communists
were bound to be cautious towards a Party which took its orders from
Moscow. Peasants wanted their own land, not the collectivisation
which was Communist policy. In August 1945 Mikolajczyk resigned
from the Government and formed a new Polish Peasant Party. Stalin
encouraged the Communists to keep negotiating with Mikolajczyk, in
view of the latter's support in the countryside. The 'Democratic Bloc'
led by the Communists was declared victorious in a referendum on
reform held in June 1946, although it was revealed in 1990 that a
majority had actually voted against the Communist proposals. In
manipulated elections in 1947, the Government Bloc officially won
394 seats and the Peasant Party only 28. Perhaps more significant was
the Communist success, repeated throughout Eastern and Central
Europe, of securing control of internal security and the police. The
Peasant Party was increasingly harassed. In October 1947
Mikolajczyk fled Poland and persecution of opposition parties began
in earnest.

Stalin's dream of a friendly buffer state on his western border was
marred only by internal disputes amongst Polish Communists.
Gomulka himself was not prepared to be a Soviet stooge. He had
already declared in 1945: 'Our party has been tempered by the hard
struggle against the German occupation, our blood and our lives are
the foundation stone of the reborn Poland. We pioneered her liberation. Blood and combat have given us the right to determine her future
and character.' His belief in a 'Polish road to Socialism' contrasted
with Stalin's concept of a closely integrated Eastern Europe.

Gomulka opposed the Soviet policy on collectivisation and was
sensitive to Polish conditions when implementing Socialism.

Consequently he was accused of 'nationalist deviation' and replaced as Party leader by Bierut in September 1948. Moscow felt securely in control and did not regard extensive purges of the Polish leadership as necessary. However, given the long history of Russo-Polish antagonism, it is scarcely surprising that Soviet-Polish relations were never to be smooth for the next 40 years.

b) Hungary

In Hungary Mátyás Rákosi's attempts to increase Communist influence were assisted by the presence of the Red Army until 1947, although as a defeated power Hungary, like Romania and Bulgaria, was subject to an Allied Control Commission. The Hungarian Communists followed a strategy of coalition, increasing their influence in the trade unions and allying with the Socialists but making no overt bid for power. The Communists had performed poorly in the 1945 elections, probably because they would not accept the idea of giving land to the peasantry. However, they now followed classic 'salami tactics' by allying with the Smallholders' Party and the Social Democrats. Although the Allied Control Commission insisted on a coalition Government, the Communists secured the Ministry of the Interior and then sought further alliances with the Socialists and the National Peasant Party in order to counteract the strength of the Smallholders. The fact that the Smallholders were themselves split only assisted the Communists in the long run.

Political in-fighting was further complicated by Soviet interference: for example, the Soviets vetoed some parliamentary bills and arrested the Smallholders' leader Bela Kovács on charges of offences against the Red Army. As in Poland, elections to parliament were rigged: in 1947 the Left Bloc of Communists and Socialists won 45 per cent of the votes. After 1947 the Communists held five of 15 Government posts.

However, Stalin could not afford to be complacent. Some Hungarian Socialists, following a trend in Western Europe, were urging a break with the Communists. Stalin was also concerned with the situation in Yugoslavia. Tito's Communists had come to power there with little direct help from the USSR and were now developing their independent brand of Communism, a cause of conflict with Stalin. Tito broke with Stalin in 1948, and thereafter Yugoslavia remained outside the Soviet fold and was a possible inspiration to other independently-minded Communist movements. The Soviets knew that there were links between the Hungarians and Yugoslavs from the War, when exiled Hungarian Communists had returned to Hungary along underground routes operated by Tito's partisans. The strength of Soviet concerns, and their power in Hungary, were demonstrated in the treatment of László Rajk, who had been leader of the underground Hungarian Communist Party from 1941. He was tried and executed in 1949. His crime, along with several colleagues, was to have collaborated with Yugoslav Communists in 'anti-Socialist activities'. The tone of repression was being set. Social Democrats who resisted pressure to amalgamate with the Communists were expelled from the Party. More Communists joined the Government, and by the time of the 1949 elections there was no opposition.

c) Romania

The process of Communist consolidation in Romania was similar though more speedy than in Hungary. Stalin felt that he had a free hand, since Romania was recognised by the West as being within the Soviet sphere of influence. After Romanian Government forces fired on a demonstration in February 1945, Stalin decided that he could not rely upon Gheorghiu-Dej alone. He ordered the Red Army to advance and forced the king to appoint a National Democratic Front Government containing two Communists. This Government arrested opponents and censored the press. Romania was policed by the Red Army.

In March 1946 the Socialists and Communists merged, and the resulting Popular Front won 80 per cent of the vote in the November elections. There was considerable popular support for the Left, since it was not associated in people's minds with the old unpopular regime. The Communists had the added security of the promise of Soviet support in the background. A Republic was proclaimed. Gheorghiu-Dej quickly established his authority by ruthlessly purging all those who disagreed with him, both inside and outside the Party. The USSR was content, counting on Gheorgiu-Dej's loyalty to Stalin.

d) Bulgaria

'Salami tactics', manipulated elections and purging of opponents were all features of the transition to Communism in Bulgaria. As in Hungary and the USSR, the indigenous Communists had to proceed cautiously at first, since Bulgaria was controlled by the Allies until a peace treaty was agreed in February 1947. However, an extensive purge was already under way. Over 30,000 representatives of the previous regime were tried. On one night in February 1945 alone, 100 leading political figures were shot.

Nikola Petkov, leader of the old Agrarian Party, refused to fight the 1945 election, and neither he nor the West would recognise the subsequent Government. Stalin still wanted Western support, so a new election was held in October 1946, dominated by complaints about electoral abuses. The Communist-dominated Fatherland Front won over 75 per cent of the votes; Petkov won 22 per cent. Once the Allied Control Commission had departed, the Communists were left to follow their own policies. Petkov was executed after a show trial, and the Agrarians were forced to become junior partners of the Communists in a nominal coalition. In April 1947 all opposition parties were outlawed. During the next few years several other Bulgarians were tried, including several priests. The Communists had no qualms about their policies, possibly because they had considerable popular support at the end of the War. They regarded themselves, as Communists did in other states, as having carried out a 'revolution from below', in the name of the people.

e) The Communist 'Coup' in Czechoslovakia

The caution which Stalin showed in his dealings with other Eastern and Central European states emerging from the War was also evident in his dealings with Czechoslovakia. The Communists had considerable support here, and they controlled the Interior Ministry. The Communist leader Gottwald spoke about a gradual approach to extending influence by working through organisations like the trade unions and by cooperating with President Beneš. Beneš himself was wary of Soviet influence and hoped to make Czechoslovakia a bridge between East and West.

Many Communists wanted a push for complete power. They already controlled the army and the police and won 39 per cent of the votes in the May 1946 election. Allied with the Socialists, they had a majority and dominated the new coalition Government. The Communists won support from the peasants by giving them land taken from the one million German inhabitants expelled from the country in 1945 and 1946. Many Party members were factory directors and the Party was well represented on local and district committees. Gottwald became Prime Minister after the election.

Gottwald's Government was unique in the Eastern Bloc: it was a freely-entered-into coalition of the former Government-in Exile and the Communist Party leadership back from Moscow. However, difficulties soon appeared. In 1947 the Czechoslovak Government announced its willingness to accept Marshall Aid, an American offer to countries recovering from the War. The USSR regarded the Marshall Plan as an anti-Soviet conspiracy and forced Gottwald to reject it. Gottwald also faced a challenge from Rudolf Slánsky, who argued for a greater say in decision-making for organisations like trade unions.

Unity was threatened. The Socialists complained when several non-Communist police officials were sacked. The Communists campaigned for a change in the electoral system, afraid that they might lose the forthcoming election of May 1948. Arguments broke out within the Government, resulting in 12 resignations. Although the Social Democrats remained on board, other parties hoped to force a showdown over the powers which the Communists were gradually assuming. At the same time they hoped that Beneš would refuse the resignations and call an election. However, although these politicians claimed that they were trying to bolster Beneš in his resistance against the Communists, they did nothing concrete to help him. The resignations turned out to be a tactical blunder, playing into the Communists' hands. There was no evidence of a concerted Communist conspiracy. However, the Communists now called for more reform 'from below'. Militant workers were organised to demonstrate. Those Socialists who refused to join the Communist Party were imprisoned. The Communists now had a majority in parliament and Beneš was manipulated into agreeing to a Communist-dominated Government from which opponents were removed.

The Communists could claim that there was some popular support for their actions, although not for the subsequent transition to one-party rule. It was certainly not necessary to take up Stalin's offer of Red Army help to ensure a Communist takeover. The transition to

a

b

a) Gottwald and colleagues at the time of the Communist takeover in February 1948. b) The same photograph as it later appeared in Communist history books, with Gottwald's colleagues, who had been purged by 1952, edited out.

Communist rule was relatively smooth, and was brought about by tactical blunders and irresolution by the opposition and Beneš, along with some popular support. However, as the Cold War developed the West looked for more sinister interpretations, such as a Soviet plot to enforce Communism wherever possible. Certainly the Soviet presence in the background was a crucial factor, but the Communists did have supporters, and to a large extent their opponents played into the Communists' hands. The interpretation of one British commentator was that 'The Communists conquered Czechoslovakia not by smashing the state machine but by taking it over from above after careful penetration' (H. Seton Watson, *The Manchester Guardian*, 4 August 1949).

After the 'coup' of February 1948 the Communists held all the key Government posts in Czechoslovakia. Representatives of other parties were selected by the Communists. One was Foreign Minister Jan Masaryk, son of the founder of Czechoslovakia. He was reported as having committed suicide in March, although there is little doubt that Soviet security forces were implicated in his death. One-party rule was now enforced. The Social Democrats merged with the Communists. Beneš resigned in June 1948 and was succeeded as President by Gottwald. The Communist Antonín Zápotocký became Prime Minister. The Communists were in control.

f) The Birth of the GDR

The experience of East German Communists was very different from elsewhere in the region for several reasons, but mostly due to the Cold War. This made Germany's division at the end of the War into Eastern and Western spheres of influence apparently permanent. The fate of Germany was bound up with Cold War tensions and international diplomacy. At the end of the War the Allies divided Germany into Soviet, American, British and French zones of occupation. Berlin, deep inside the Soviet zone, was also divided into four zones, run by an Allied Control Commission. At this stage there was no intention of formally dividing Germany into separate nations. The USSR's main concerns were to establish an anti-fascist administration in its zone, destroy the legacy of Nazism and extract reparations from Germany.

Political parties re-emerged in Germany: the Communists (KPD), Social Democrats (SPD), Christian Democrats (CDU) and Liberal Democrats (LDP). Later there were the National Democratic Party (NDPD) and the Peasants' Party (DBD). In the Eastern zone these parties formed a National Front, controlled by the Communists. The more popular SPD was in 1946 forcibly merged with the KPD to form the Socialist Unity Party (SED), which ruled for the next 40 years. Because elections later in 1946 did not give the Communists a mandate, in subsequent elections voters were only presented with an approved list of candidates, and most Social Democrat members of the SED were soon purged.

One thing was clear: Stalin saw his zone as part of the spoils of war. He was determined both that Germany should never threaten the USSR again and that there should be a friendly government in power. As Cold War tensions developed, Berlin became a flashpoint in 1948. The Soviets tried to force the West out of Berlin by blockading it. The West retained its presence in Berlin by means of a massive airlift of supplies. The formation of NATO (North Atlantic Treaty Organisation) was one response to this crisis. Following its settlement, with the West still in West Berlin, the democratic Federal Republic of Germany was formed out of lands controlled by the Western Allies. The German Democratic Republic (GDR) was formed in the East in 1949. Most of its economic assets were taken to the USSR as reparations for the War.

However, it was many years before the Soviets were committed to the idea of a separate East German state. Stalin kept his options open. He could not tolerate a strong, potentially threatening Germany. On the other hand, a weak, divided state might become a drain on Soviet resources and might be attracted to the wealthier West. Those German Communists who had survived Hitler's regime had no doubts that their country had legitimate status as the only genuinely 'anti-fascist state'. This claim had some justice, since the denazification process by which former Nazis were purged was less thorough in West Germany than in the East. Yet after Stalin's death in 1953 the new Soviet leadership considered dissolving the GDR as a contribution towards reducing East-West tensions. The West rejected the Soviet suggestion of a neutral Germany in 1955. Thereafter the Soviet position hardened, and in 1955 Khrushchev gave his unconditional backing to the East German regime, soon afterwards recognising the West German state also. By then the East German Communists had been firmly in control for several years, and their leader Walter Ulbricht was keen for East Germans to be seen as allies of the USSR in their own right rather than as a possible bargaining tool in Cold War diplomacy.

Other Communist states in the emerging Eastern Bloc had long been nation states in their own right. Even after its establishment, the GDR retained some distinctive features: one was that it had 300,000 Soviet troops permanently stationed on its territory. Although these troops were part of the Eastern Bloc's deployment against NATO, most historians have also taken this as evidence that the GDR's existence only rested on the power of the USSR, at least in its early years.

g) Assessment

So by 1949 Communists were securely in control in all the countries which are the focus of this book. They benefited from several factors. In those countries that had been under German occupation, Communists from 1941 onwards had played a prominent part in the anti-Nazi resistance. This won them support from some non-Communist voters and gave them a moral claim to have an important say in any postwar political arrangements made within individual countries. The Communists also benefited from the popular mood for change present in most countries throughout Europe at the end of the War. The hardship and endurance of the war years bred a radical mood. There was a desire for, or at least acceptance of, social change, and this increased support for left-wing political parties. The Communists certainly gained support which in most cases had been lacking before the War, except perhaps in Czechoslovakia.

The Communist Party leaders were committed hard-working individuals, who had no experience of government but had experienced long political apprenticeships in difficult conditions, often including spells in prison or the resistance. Many of them had also had training in Moscow in the arts of political infighting, which gave them a distinct advantage against more 'traditional' party leaders. Above all there was the presence of the USSR, which although having suffered greatly during the War, emerged from it as a great European power under a determined leader. The Red Army had either occupied territory and now controlled it, as in the case of East Germany, or was in the background, ready to give practical support to Communist leaders in other countries should they need it in their quest for sole power or coalition with other left-wing groups. With the Communists holding these advantages, other politicians had in most cases no answer to the infiltrationist tactics of the Communists, who either worked on their own or through Popular Fronts.

The less attractive features of authoritarianism were quickly in place. The regimes were now in a position to establish structures of power and formulate social and economic policies in line with those long in place in Stalin's USSR.

Working on 'The Communist Takeover, 1945-48'

In compiling your notes, concentrate on acquiring an understanding of the key points. What were the main developments in the Eastern Bloc during this period? How was Communism established in the various countries? Were there similarities and differences in the process in different countries? What part did the USSR play in the process? What advantages did the Communists have over other parties? How popular were the Communists?

Answering structured questions and essay questions on 'The Communist Takeover, 1945-48'

Examination questions on Eastern and Central Europe may well be general questions on the whole region, which enable you to bring to bear your knowledge of several countries to reinforce your answer. Other questions may relate to specific countries, usually requiring you to make a comparison between particular states, or those of your choice. Questions will not require you to know the detail of every event which happened, but they will expect acquaintance with the main events, personalities and trends during this period. Questions will sometimes be divided into two parts, the first requiring a factual account, the second requiring a more analytical approach to a specified problem.

A typical question is:

a) Outline the process by which the Communists acquired power in any *two* of the following countries after the Second World War: Poland; Czechoslovakia; Hungary; Romania; Bulgaria.

b) Compare and contrast the reasons for the Communists' success in gaining power in the two countries of your choice.

The key words in the first part of the question are *'Outline the process'*. The parameters are clear: you are being asked to describe the main events between the end of the War and about 1948/9. You should outline the main stages of the Communist takeover in the countries you have chosen.

The second part of the question is more demanding, because the answer demands analytical skills. You will focus on the two countries of your choice, and the key words are *'compare and contrast'*. In other words, do not deal with each case in isolation, but make a genuine comparison of the two. For example, was Soviet influence more important in one country than another? Did the Communists have more support in one country than another? Was the nature of the Communist 'coup' in Czechoslovakia in 1948 significantly different from, say, the Soviet intervention in Poland? Analyse *why* the processes occurred as much as *how* they occurred.

Summary Diagram

3 Stalinist Europe and Regional Organisations

POINTS TO CONSIDER

This chapter will examine the methods by which the Communist regimes maintained their power in Central and Eastern Europe for two generations after their formation, and also their links with the USSR and with each other. Your aim in reading the chapter should be in particular to understand the repressive nature of the Stalinist regimes. Then you should try to appreciate the role of the Warsaw Pact and COMECON and the extent to which these organisations exerted a positive influence throughout the period of Communist domination. Chapter 6 will examine opposition to the regimes and the response to that opposition.

KEY DATES

1947 Introduction of Marshall Plan
1949 Formation of NATO
       Creation of COMECON
1955 Warsaw Pact signed
1956 Intervention of Warsaw Pact in Hungary
1968 Intervention of Warsaw Pact in Czechoslovakia
       Announcement of Brezhnev Doctrine
1991 Dissolution of Warsaw Pact

1 The Basis of Communist Power

> **KEY ISSUE** How did the Communist regimes exert control in what were essentially one-party states?

There were common features to the exercise of power throughout the Eastern Bloc. The regimes were police states: the secret police, modelled on the Soviet KGB and reinforced by an army of informers, exercised surveillance and kept overt opposition to a minimum. Mass participation in elections was encouraged: the results were manipulated if necessary, but in any case usually only 'official' candidates were permitted to stand for election. Control of the media and education, reinforced by propaganda machines, was used to try to influence minds. There would be stage-managed parades and rituals. Personality cults developed around the leaders, although only Ceauşescu's in Romania was to rival Stalin's own cult.

A single party ruled, although other satellite parties might be permitted as a democratic facade. Due to the nature of politics in the aftermath of the Second World War, Popular or National Fronts operated in all the Eastern Bloc states, although after 1950 Hungary and Romania were single-party states with a party list of candidates at elections. In the other states there were other loyal parties besides the Communists, and their share of parliamentary seats would be determined in advance of elections. The GDR (East Germany) provided an example of a nominally 'democratic' multi-party system. Here the lower of two parliamentary houses contained several parties, which were permitted to act as the mouthpiece of the Communist Socialist Unity Party (SED). This was a Communist ploy: for example, because the Communists had little support amongst the peasantry the SED formed the Peasant Party to present its policies in rural areas, on the assumption that peasants would find the regime's policies more palatable if put across by their 'own' party, even if in reality it was controlled by the SED.

The ruling parties took the Soviet version of Marxism-Leninism, with its belief in an ultimately classless society, as their ideal. Despite the official belief in the eventual success of a worldwide Communist revolution, the Eastern Bloc states did not pursue expansionist foreign policies on their own account: instead they slavishly followed the dictates of Soviet foreign policy, with Romania as the notable exception. In so far as there was an agreed foreign policy among the various states, it emphasised friendship with the USSR and deliberately played down nationalist feeling.

There were several similarities between the constitutional arrangements of the Eastern Bloc states after 1950. They had constitutions modelled on the Soviet one, and these usually referred to the leading role of the Party. There were parliaments, mostly consisting of one chamber (Czechoslovakia had two after 1969), but they met rarely. Much of the decision-making was done by Presidiums or Councils of State, which could issue decrees. Like the Councils, the presidents and heads of state were appointed by parliament. Parliaments also appointed Councils of Ministers, whose chairmen acted as Prime Ministers. These arrangements appeared to give the parliaments considerable power, but this was on paper only. Parliaments were not elected democratically: candidates were normally selected by the ruling Party, and there was no real choice for the voter, so that elections were simply the opportunity for regimes to mobilise the population in a show of apparent support for themselves.

Conformity could not be taken for granted. In Poland Catholicism was a powerful force which competed with the regime for the hearts and minds of the people. The Polish Government separated church and state after the War and nationalised church lands, but this only strengthened popular support for the church, the more so when the regime imprisoned the influential Cardinal Wyszynski. Gomulka released the Cardinal and signed a concordat with the church. However, there were further problems: religious teaching was banned from schools in 1961, then reinstated, a unique position in the Eastern

Bloc. This new reconciliation was ended in 1978 when Karol Wojtyla, Metropolitan of Cracow, was elected Pope John Paul II. He became a focus for Polish national feeling. In East Germany it was the Lutheran Church which acted as a focus for popular dissatisfaction.

At the highest level Soviet embassies ensured that the USSR was well informed about all activities within client states, whilst many of the region's leaders had received their ideological training in Moscow. The USSR exercised its influence in the Eastern Bloc in a variety of ways: through Russian being taught in schools; through employing Soviet-trained personnel in key positions, particularly those involving security; and through to a large extent isolating one Eastern Bloc state from another, despite all the propaganda about 'Socialist brotherhood'. At lower levels membership of the Party was a pre-requisite for influence. The Soviet *Nomenklatura* system was adopted: this consisted of lists of the Party faithful from whom leaders and administrators were plucked when the need arose.

Party structures were broadly similar in the various countries. There was a pyramid of organisations. At the lowest level, local party organisations elected intermediate organisations, which in turn elected government organisations. These in turn appointed the Central Committee, which was the executive; a Politburo, which determined policy; and a Secretariat, which managed party organisation and discipline. Leading figures in the Government would always be Communist Party members. There were no rival organisations, and the Party infiltrated every walk of life. Every workplace had a Party cell, and every organisation had Party approval or a Party representative. Because the regimes believed in centralised political control, the Party tended to take over other government and administrative functions. There were Communist youth movements, although Poland also permitted a scout movement. The majority of Party members engaged in formal Party activities in their spare time, but there was a much smaller number of full-time Party *apparatchiks*, or officials, from whom the leadership was drawn. Bureaucracies expanded: for example, administrative personnel made up well over ten per cent of the workforces of Hungary and Czechoslovakia.

Cultural policy was determined by the dictates of Marxism-Leninism and Soviet influence. There were official organisations for friendship with the USSR and to promote peace. Soviet books and films were imported. Soviet and Socialist holidays replaced national public holidays. However, after Stalin's death, local expressions of cultural identity such as folk festivals were allowed, apart from when there were periodic attempts to promote a 'national identity', notably in Romania and Bulgaria. The regimes tried to control the various churches by setting up government agencies over them, with the ultimate ambition of making religion redundant. In the meantime, church activities were usually allowed, although churches were harrassed in Romania and Czechoslovakia. However, discouragement did not destroy religious belief, and in Poland in particular it remained a potent force to rival the official ideology of 'actually existing Socialism'.

Ultimately regimes were kept in power by oppression reinforced by propaganda. In Romania the regime gained a particular reputation for repression. However, Communist regimes elsewhere relied to some extent on an unwritten social contract whereby populations were promised rising living standards in return for at least outward conformity. In the background was the threat of Soviet intervention should a regime feel seriously threatened or should that regime itself show signs of departing too far from orthodoxy.

Although there were major challenges to the system in Hungary, Czechoslovakia and Poland, and there were disagreements over ideology and policy within Communist Parties, Communist control was secure for almost 40 years. Two factors eventually broke the mould. The first was a growing awareness that Communist regimes could neither deliver their economic and social promises nor count any longer on the mass compliance of subject populations. Secondly, there was a radical change in the USSR of the 1980s: there a regime beset by its own problems and undergoing controversial reforms made clear its unwillingness to come to the aid of threatened regimes in its client states.

2 Repression

> **KEY ISSUE** What was the importance of repression as practised by the Communist regimes, and how effective was it?

Power ultimately depended upon force. By 1950 the Polish Party had over 1.2 million members, kept in line by purges. There were 97 concentration camps identified in Poland by the early 1950s. There were periodic clampdowns on dissent from outside the Party. Several Polish intellectuals and students were imprisoned in the 1960s for criticising official policies, whilst Polish Jews, a traditional scapegoat, were harassed. In 1968, a student demonstration in Warsaw was suppressed: it broke out in support of Czech reformers and in response to the closure of a nineteenth century play containing the provocative line 'the only things Moscow sends us are jackasses, idiots and spies.'

Czechoslovakia provided an example of direct Soviet involvement in enforcing conformity within the Party, which contained almost 1.5 million members by 1954. The USSR knew that arms were being supplied via Czechoslovakia to the new state of Israel, with which the Soviets were on bad terms. Stalin also suspected that Titoist agents were operating in Czechoslovakia. Extensive purges followed: over half the Central Committee and six of the seven Central Committee Secretaries were removed. Half a million of Czechoslovakia's Party members were purged, many ending up in the 124 concentration camps. Soviet 'consultants' helped organise trials. Even after destalini-sation began in the USSR in the mid 1950s, the Czech leadership would not liberalise or deviate from the Stalinist model.

Communist consolidation in Hungary was also reinforced by repression. In the early 1950s 200,000 Party members were purged, many ending up in the 199 concentration camps. The Hungarian Party contained 864,000 members by 1954, in comparison with 1.2 million in 1949. A prominent victim of Rákosi's obsession with repres-sion was Janos Kádár, jailed for four years in 1951 for treason and espionage. Major purges followed the suppression of the 1956 Rising. There was a similar picture in East Germany, where the secret police, the military and the Party worked together more closely than in any other Eastern Bloc state, including the USSR itself. Already by 1950 there had been arrests and show trials to root out possible dissenters and to enforce conformity. The GDR's State Security Service (the *Stasi*) was formed in 1950. By 1989 it had over 100,000 paid employees with the task of 'preventing or throttling at the earliest stages - using whatever means and methods may be necessary - all attempts to delay or to hinder the victory of socialism.' It also employed over 200,000 informers. An outward conformity at least as great as that which had existed in Hitler's Germany now prevailed in the Communist GDR. At a higher level, Ulbricht purged his more moderate rivals: by 1954 about two-thirds of members of regional committees had been replaced. The SED contained about 1.4 million members in 1954, compared with 2 million in 1947.

Rigid conformity was always enforced by the hardline regimes of Romania and Bulgaria. Gheorghiu-Dej purged potential rivals, whilst his successor Nicolae Ceauşescu earned a reputation as one of the most ruthless leaders in the Eastern Bloc. His power, reinforced by the large secret police force, the *Securitate*, was never seriously threatened before his fall. In Bulgaria Todor Zhivkov purged his rivals during the 1960s.

3 The Warsaw Pact

> **KEY ISSUE** What was the purpose of the Warsaw Pact and what was its significance for the regimes of the region?

The Warsaw Pact and COMECON were two other means by which the regimes, and more specifically the USSR, attempted to exercise control over internal policy and impose unity throughout the region for political, defence and economic ends. This was not always achieved, and these organisations created occasional disagreements between the regimes. This was particularly true of the Warsaw Pact, commonly perceived in the West as a vehicle for Soviet domination over its client states as much as a means for strengthening Soviet military capability.

a) The Origins of the Warsaw Pact

The Warsaw Pact arose from Soviet security concerns as the Cold War developed. Having friendly neighbours was important to Stalin as a means of increasing Soviet ability to resist economic, political and military pressure from the West. From 1948 Eastern Bloc regimes signed bilateral military treaties with the USSR. The admission of West Germany into the North Atlantic Treaty Organisation (NATO) in 1955 alarmed the Eastern Bloc, since NATO was the bedrock of Western defence policy in Europe. The USSR was concerned at the prospect of being surrounded by anti-Communist alliances, whilst the other Eastern Bloc regimes had their own concerns: if the Cold War ever hotted up, their countries would probably be in the firing line. A nuclear war would be catastrophic, but even a conventional, non-nuclear conflict between the superpowers was likely to be fought in Central Europe.

The Warsaw Pact Treaty was signed in the Polish capital on 14 May 1955 by the USSR, Albania, Bulgaria, East Germany, Hungary, Poland, Czechoslovakia and Romania. The preamble referred to concerns over West German integration into Western Europe and the need to counterbalance NATO. The signatories committed themselves to specific and sometimes overlapping political and military clauses:

1   The contracting parties:
    Confirm once again their striving for the creation of a system of collective security in Europe based on the participation of all European states, irrespective of their social or state structure ... taking into
5   consideration at the same time the situation which has arisen in Europe as the result of the ratification of the Paris agreements envisaging the formation of a new military alignment in the form of the West European Union with the participation of Western Germany, which is being militarised, and her inclusion in the North Atlantic Bloc, which increases the
10 danger of a new war and creates a threat to the national security of peace-loving states ...
    Guided by the aims and principles of the United Nations Charter, in the interests of the further strengthening and developing of friendship, collaboration and mutual assistance in accordance with the principles
15 of respecting the independence and sovereignty of the states and non-interference in their internal affairs [there follows a list of specific clauses] ...
    In the event of a system of collective security being set up in Europe and a pact to this effect being signed - to which each party to this treaty
20 will direct its efforts - the present treaty will lapse from the day such a collective security treaty comes into force.

Signatories agreed to settle international disputes by peaceful means, seek disarmament, cooperate in economic and cultural activities, and work for a general European treaty of collective security. They also agreed not to interfere in each other's internal affairs, including ideological issues. Therefore the intervention of Warsaw Pact forces in Hungary in 1956 and Czechoslovakia in 1968, on the grounds that Socialism was under threat and counter-revolution beckoned, could not be justified by the terms of the Alliance, despite claims often made at the time.

The Warsaw Pact signatories also promised mutual assistance in the event of threats or attacks against individual members. The Alliance would only be invoked if there were 'an armed attack in Europe.' The Treaty was to last initially for 20 years, and it was renewed for another 20 in April 1985. There was no specifically ideological basis to the Alliance, and therefore in theory it was open to any state to join. Security was supplemented by separate bilateral agreements between the USSR and its allies allowing for the stationing of Soviet troops in Eastern Bloc countries.

b) The Operation of the Warsaw Pact

The Warsaw Pact was not a monolithic, totally united organisation, and its nature changed during the course of its existence. There were disagreements amongst the Soviets from the start about whether it was primarily a means of strengthening the military security of the entire Eastern Bloc or whether its political aspects were more important. In its early days it was sometimes mooted that the Pact might be bargained away in return for concessions from the West, such as the abolition of NATO. Contradictory statements were made about the role of the Alliance. Some Soviet generals referred to defending the 'gains of socialism', although this was not among the stated aims of the Treaty and added ammunition to those who claimed that the Pact was chiefly regarded as a guarantor of the existing political system rather than a means of territorial defence. This was also an interpretation put on the Pact by some Western analysts such as Christopher Jones (in *Soviet Influence in Eastern Europe - Political Autonomy and the Warsaw Pact*, Praeger 1981). He argued that the political purpose of the Pact was paramount and that integration was designed to prevent Eastern Bloc countries from even attempting to rely upon themselves for their own defence. Instead, the argument ran, they would be conditioned to rely upon Soviet help against external threats and would become politically dependent on the USSR. It might also be necessary for these countries to call upon Soviet force to protect their regimes from enemies within. However, Eastern and Central Europe was important to the Soviets' own defence, and therefore the Alliance had a definite military rationale, whatever the political ramifications.

Member states were sometimes wary of the political implications of the Alliance. Ceaușescu's Romania refused to participate in the 1968 invasion of Czechoslovakia. During debates about *détente* in the 1970s, Pact members were concerned that the USSR was not taking into account their own national interests when discussing possible alterations in the deployment of military forces in Europe. Soviet plans to deploy SS-20 missiles in Eastern and Central Europe would have placed the host nations even more directly in the firing line of any European war. Member states were not always consulted by the USSR, and they were concerned by Soviet insistence on high levels of military spending. The Soviet signing of the Helsinki Agreements on Human Rights forced some Eastern Bloc regimes on to the defensive over their own records. The USSR did not consult its Allies before invading Afghanistan.

Tensions were sometimes created by the fact that the Soviets were clearly the controlling presence in the Warsaw Pact, although sensitive to criticism, they increased opportunities for consultation in the decades after 1955. The Commander-in-Chief of the Joint Forces and the Chief of General Staff were always to be Soviet. The Eastern Bloc Governments, except the GDR, exercised authority over their own armies in peacetime. However, it seems likely that, in the event of war, the Soviets would have taken over all important political and military decision-making, since they regarded the Eastern Bloc as vital to their own defence. Although Eastern Bloc armies were equipped with systems capable of carrying nuclear warheads, available evidence suggests that only Soviet personnel would have had the authority to employ them. By implication this meant that Eastern Bloc governments would have had little or no say in when a conventional war might escalate into nuclear conflict, even when fought over their own territory. The Czechoslovak, Romanian and East German Governments all expressed concerns to the USSR on this point.

Soviet dominance was also evident in the make-up of conventional forces. The ratio of troops from Eastern Bloc states to Soviet troops was usually around 1:4 in favour of the latter (whereas in NATO the ratio between the USA and its European allies was 2:3). The assumption was that a major military confrontation would be in Germany, and therefore Poland, the GDR and Czechoslovakia were regarded as the key allies of the USSR. Poland had the largest army of the Eastern Bloc, but East Germany's was regarded as the most efficient. A relatively small contingent of Red Army troops was stationed in Poland, in an attempt to avoid antagonism with an historically anti-Russian population. Hungary had the smallest Eastern Bloc army, matched by an equal number of Soviet troops. Czechoslovakian forces were sharply reduced in strength after the 1968 crisis. There were no Soviet troops in Bulgaria, because it was regarded as a stable and loyal ally. Romania had a small army, had no border with a NATO state, and was half-hearted in its commitment to the concept of common defence. Therefore the Red Army had no presence in Romania and its forces were not subject to Warsaw Pact command; nor did it participate in the regular military exercises which the Pact held, particularly from 1961.

Member states were fully represented on the various organs of the

Warsaw Treaty Organisation (WTO). The Political Consultative Committee (PCC) met 22 times between 1955 and 1982, and then annually, in order to discuss any problems which arose. It made recommendations on the foreign policy to be adopted by member states and appointed to key positions in the Alliance. In 1969 a Committee of Defence Ministers (CDM) was set up. The Joint Command (JC), which integrated the forces of member states into the Joint Armed Forces, and the Joint Armed Forces (JAFS) were stationed in Moscow. In 1976 a Committee of Foreign Ministers (CFM) was set up for 'further perfection of the mechanism of political cooperation within the framework of the Treaty.' This was in response to member states pressing the USSR for more consultation.

It is difficult to determine both the exact extent to which the Warsaw Pact acted as a unifying force amongst Eastern Bloc states and the extent to which the USSR or its client states gained most from its existence. The USSR was able to involve member states in major actions and thereby try to give the impression that controversial actions such as the invasion of Hungary and Czechoslovakia were widely supported in the Socialist world - although these actions were always perceived in the West as initiated by the Soviets anyway. In 1956 the Soviets cited the Warsaw Treaty as justification for their intervention in Hungary, but the military operation was conducted outside the Alliance. The reality was that Soviet actions directly contravened the Treaty's insistence on non-interference in the internal affairs of member states. Possibly because of this, the USSR later tried to weld the Alliance more closely together, by staging joint military exercises and bringing officers from different countries to Moscow to be trained as an élite group with loyalties to 'Socialism' rather than to individual states.

In the invasion of Czechoslovakia in 1968 the Soviets employed East German, Polish, Hungarian and Bulgarian troops as well as their own. The USSR did this not out of need but to avoid the impression that intervention was solely a Soviet affair. After the invasion the Soviets issued the 'Warsaw Letter', which emphasised the need for collective action to protect Socialism. The Brezhnev Doctrine also justified intervention on similar grounds. These steps would legitimise actions technically prohibited by the Warsaw Treaty. Even so, the strains which such actions created made the Alliance, and the USSR in particular, even more keen to negotiate or even compromise in later crises rather than use force. This was noticeable in 1980-81, when there were rumours that the USSR was threatening to invade Poland if General Jaruzelski did not act decisively to avert the collapse of Communist authority. The reality was that the Soviets were reluctant to invade because of international repercussions, because of the likelihood of opposition from the Polish Army and because other members of the Alliance would have been very uneasy at military involvement.

Perceptions of the role of the Alliance underwent other changes during its life. An early simplistic Western view of the Alliance was that Stalin was simply waiting for an opportunity to use the Alliance to invade Western Europe. More credible perhaps was the view that Stalin was implicitly threatening a massive conventional invasion of NATO territory should the West consider launching a nuclear strike against the USSR. Later strategic thinking was more sophisticated, in response to NATO's theory of 'Flexible Response', which implied that a war might be fought at varying levels of intensity without necessarily involving massive nuclear exchanges from the start. However, this was of little comfort to Central and Eastern European states which would have been the battleground for a 'conventional' war.

c) The Decline of the Warsaw Pact

It is difficult to gauge what popular feelings about the Warsaw Pact were in the member states. At a higher level there were occasional tensions between member states, as when Hungary protested to Romania about its treatment of ethnic Hungarians in Transylvania. Nevertheless, with the exception of Czechoslovakia in 1968, there is little evidence that Eastern Bloc regimes - even Romania with its independent foreign policy - wished to leave the Alliance. The regimes wanted to protect their own interests and did not always want to be dictated to by the USSR; on the other hand, they enjoyed the military security, continuity and stability promised by the Alliance.

The Alliance lost much of its rationale in the 1980s. Soviet leader Gorbachev's 'New Thinking' in foreign policy put more emphasis on flexibility and compromise in international relations and on a commitment to disarmament. The Warsaw Pact regimes had been involved in Arms Control negotiations with the West since the early 1970s. However, despite concerns about the strains on resources, there had been a reluctance to reduce large armies which were seen as a counterbalance to the technological superiority of NATO's forces. These issues seemed less crucial in the mid 1980s. Most Eastern Bloc leaders welcomed the prospect of some demilitarisation in Central Europe and the opportunity to follow their own diplomatic initiatives, for example with West Germany. As the USSR underwent major internal changes and Cold War tensions evaporated, the rationale for the Warsaw Pact quickly disappeared. In 1990 NATO declared that it no longer regarded the Warsaw Pact states as potential enemies. The Pact dissolved itself in March 1991. Views differ as to whether the Pact had contributed to stability by deterring war, or had been an expensive and wasted exercise for members of the Eastern Bloc.

4 COMECON

KEY ISSUE How important was COMECON in the economic history of the Central and Eastern European region?

a) The Purposes of COMECON

The Warsaw Pact was one unifying factor in the Eastern Bloc, at least for some of its existence. Another was COMECON (or CMEA), the Commission for Mutual Economic Aid. It was created in January 1949 by the USSR, Poland, Czechoslovakia, Romania, Hungary and Bulgaria, and later joined by some non-European Communist states. It was seen in the West as the USSR's answer to the Marshall Plan of 1947, by which the USA gave vast amounts of economic assistance to countries recovering from the devastation of the Second World War. The Soviets did refer in the communiqué setting up COMECON to the planning of 'broader economic cooperation between the peoples of the people's democracies and the Soviet Union' because 'these countries do not consider it possible to subordinate themselves to the dictates of the Marshall Plan, as this plan infringes on the sovereignty of countries and the interests of their national economies'.

The purposes and principles of COMECON were outlined in two clauses:

i   1 The purpose of the Commission for Mutual Economic Assistance is to promote, by uniting and coordinating the efforts of the member countries of the Commission, *the further deepening and perfecting of cooperation and the development of socialist economic integration*, the planned
5   development of the national economies and the acceleration of the economic and technical progress of those countries, the raising of the level of industrialisation of the countries with a less-developed industry, a continual growth in the productivity, *the gradual approximation and equalisation of the levels of economic development*, together with a steady
10 increase in the wellbeing of the peoples, of the member countries of the Commission.
2 The Commission for Mutual Economic Assistance is based on the principle of the sovereign equality of all the member countries of the Commission. Economic and scientific-technical cooperation between
15 the member countries of the Commission shall take place in accordance with the principles of *socialist internationalism, on the basis of respect for state sovereignty, independence and national interest, non-interference in the internal affairs of countries*, complete equality of rights, mutual advantage and friendly mutual aid.

COMECON therefore had both economic and political aims. However, as an organisation it was virtually inactive until 1954 when the Secretariat was set up. Whilst Stalin was alive countries concentrated on their own economic planning. The formal structures of COMECON were only agreed in 1959, and thereafter there was more substantial activity.

Khrushchev advocated 'socialist division of labour', with each member state concentrating on those areas of economic activity in which it was most efficient. This concept was built into COMECON statutes in 1962. Khrushchev declared:

1   It is impossible to develop everything everywhere simultaneously ... Hungarians, Poles, Romanians and the others have to build up everything by themselves ... As regards tractor or motor vehicle production for example, the situation today is that tractors and motor vehicles are
5   produced not only in the Soviet Union, but by Poland, Czechoslovakia, Hungary and Romania. Thus production is not always profitable. The sooner and the better we develop the division of labour between our countries, the stronger will our economies be.

b) COMECON in Action

COMECON coordinated Five-Year Plans, encouraged specialisation within national economies and sought cooperation in production, especially in chemicals and engineering. The Soviets wanted the GDR to concentrate on industrial production, whilst other states would concentrate more on agriculture, since food supplies were always a priority for the USSR. However, states like Romania argued that it was more Marxist to develop an industrial base and large working class, and had no wish to become dependent on the USSR for industrial goods. There were plans for a common transport network, an oil pipeline and an electric grid system throughout the Eastern Bloc, but most economic arrangements were made between states on a bilateral basis. When in the 1980s states moved towards a more market-orientated approach to the economy, recognising the importance of supply and demand, the prospect of coordinated economic direction seemed even less appealing.

Clearly COMECON members were not equal partners, and the USSR dominated the organisation, with its key personnel and the principal organisations concentrated in Moscow. The USSR operated a pricing system favourable to itself, although it did provide credit to member states and gave access to Soviet raw materials and energy supplies. In return, COMECON states offered manufactured products to the USSR. The terms of trade were increasingly in the USSR's favour after 1971, when Brezhnev began attempts to integrate Eastern Bloc economies more closely. Soviet dominance was ironic given that some states, for example Czechoslovakia, had more advanced economies than the Soviet one. In 1988 COMECON agreed on the 'collective concept of the international socialist division of labour.' But by then the Communist regimes were crumbling and Poland, Czechoslovakia and Hungary were keen to wind up the organisation. New regimes were more interested in cultivating closer economic ties with the West, avoiding commitment to Russia, and dealing individually with each other. COMECON had not proved noticeably successful in eliminating competition between member states or in stimulating economic growth. Its disappearance caused little stir or regret.

5 Conformity and Unity

> **KEY ISSUE** To what extent did the Eastern Bloc states conform to a pattern in terms of internal controls and external relations with each other, and how effective were the institutions?

As this chapter has demonstrated, there were several common features in the structures and practices of the Eastern Bloc states. They were all police states, although the East German security system was probably the most efficient, whilst the exercise of power was probably most arbitrary in Romania. All the regimes controlled the media and manipulated elections, although some, like the GDR with its tolerance of different parties, created the façade of pluralism. In all the states, the Communists exerted ultimate power, although the extent to which force was used against opponents within and without the Party, or non-Party institutions like churches were subjected to pressure, varied from state to state and from time to time. The structure of the Communist Parties themselves, based very much on the Soviet model as they were, did not vary in substance.

In terms of external relations, the two organisations of the Warsaw Pact and COMECON imposed a kind of unity throughout the Eastern Bloc. However, the key factor in these organisations was their subordination for most of their existence to the interests of the USSR. The Warsaw Pact was regarded as a key to the defence of Central Europe against the West, but its structures and practices sometimes created tensions between the USSR and other member states, in particular Romania. Since it was never used in anger against an external threat, we cannot ultimately judge the effectiveness of the alliance The COMECON organisation was set up for more peaceful purposes, and it did to some extent promote trade between member states. However, it never played as important a role in inter-state relations as, for example, the European Union did in the West, and certainly the economic benefits it brought to the region did not compensate for the economic weaknesses analysed in Chapter 5.

Making notes on 'Stalinist Europe and Regional Organisations'

In compiling your notes, concentrate on acquiring knowledge and understanding of some of the key features of the Eastern Bloc states from the late 1940s onwards. You should consider the role of Communist parties and all the apparatus of propaganda and force which they used to maintain power, and where possible make a comparison between the experiences of different countries. You should also consider the importance of the Warsaw Pact and COMECON as unifying factors in the region. The role of the political leaders in the Eastern Bloc, and advice on answering essays on the nature of power in the Eastern Bloc, are dealt with in Chapter 4.

Source-based questions on 'Stalinist Europe and Regional Organisations'

Read the extracts from the Warsaw Pact Treaty on page 32 and the Charter setting up COMECON on pages 37, and then answer the following questions:

1. What reasons are given in the extract from the Warsaw Treaty for the setting up of the Warsaw Pact? (4 marks)
2. Identify the elements of propaganda in both sources. (5 marks)
3. To what extent were the provisions enshrined in these extracts actually carried out after the Warsaw Treaty Organisation and COMECON came into existence? (6 marks)
4. What reservations might you have about these sources as evidence for the motivation behind the setting up of both organisations? (5 marks)

Summary Diagram

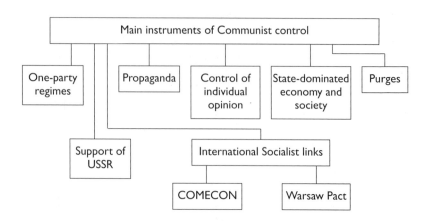

4 Leadership and Politics in the Eastern Bloc

POINTS TO CONSIDER

This chapter will focus upon the leaders of the Eastern Bloc countries and their policies during the period between the consolidation of Communist power at the end of the 1940s through to the mid 1980s, just before the collapse of the Communist regimes. Your aim on first reading this chapter should be to understand the nature of the policies which were introduced in the various countries and the degree to which they were successful or otherwise.

KEY DATES

1953 Death of Stalin
Demonstrations in East Germany crushed
1955 Warsaw Pact signed
Nagy deposed in Hungary
1956 Workers' riots in Poland
Gomulka restored to leadership
Hungarian Rising crushed
Beginnings of Destalinisation
1961 Construction of Berlin Wall
1964 Principle of New Economic Mechanism accepted in Hungary
1968 Dubček replaced Novotný as Czechoslovakian leader
Prague Spring and invasion of Czechoslovakia
Declaration of Brezhnev Doctrine
1970 Riots in Poland and dismissal of Gomulka
1971 Honecker replaced Ulbricht as GDR leader
1976 Strikes and demonstrations in Poland
1980 Unrest in Poland and creation of *Solidarity*
1981 Declaration of martial law in Poland

The dominant role of Communist Parties in the Eastern Bloc was outlined in Chapter 3. Also crucially important in maintaining Communist power was the role of the Party leaders. Sometimes they have been portrayed in the main as grey, rather uninspiring figures, subservient to Moscow and relying ultimately for their survival on controlling the levers of the one-party police state. However, there were differences as well as similarities in their approaches to power. Although men like Walter Ulbricht in the GDR presented an austere character to the outside world, these were leaders who on the whole had gone through long and often difficult apprenticeships, were members of small and usually illegal parties before the Second World War, were frequently imprisoned, and were frequently active in the resistance against Germany during the War. Although committed to a common Marxist ideology, they were not immune to the particular national interests of their own countries. Some like Ceauşescu became personally corrupt, and long-standing leaders like Zhivkov in Bulgaria found it difficult to respond to demands for change in the late 1980s in time to save themselves and their parties. But for many years, these leaders and their regimes were crucial in dictating the course of events in the Eastern Bloc.

1 Gomulka and Poland

> **KEY ISSUE**   What was the nature of Gomulka's policies inside Poland and why were they ultimately unsuccessful?

In Poland Gomulka put his individual stamp on the development of Communism. Following riots in Poznan in 1956, prompted by workers protesting against their conditions, Gomulka made a come-back as leader. He represented the reformist wing of the Party and had to overcome opposition from a group of prominent hardliners called the Natolin Group (named after a village near Warsaw). Political uncertainties provoked fears of Soviet intervention and led to a visit to Warsaw by Khrushchev. However, as a member of the Polish Politburo later declared: 'From the start, we took the view that this was an internal matter for our Party and its Central Committee. We did everything to calm down our Soviet comrades. We tried to explain the essence, the sense of democratisation, now in course, and the impossibility for it to be reversed.'

Gomulka, once elected, promised change. He told the Central Committee:

1   The workers of Poznan did not rebel against People's Poland, or against Socialism, they protested against the evil which got into our social system and which offended them deeply … It would be politically naive to try to present this tragedy as the work of imperialist forces and of
5   provocateurs. The causes of the Poznan tragedy, of the profound dissat-isfaction of our working class, lie in us, in the leadership of the Party, in the government … The loss of the confidence of the working class means the loss of the moral basis of power … We must tell the working class the painful truth. We cannot afford at the present moment any
10 considerable increase of wages …
      The mapping out of the Russian road to socialism passed gradually from the hands of the Central Committee into the hands of an even smaller group of people, and finally became the monopoly of Stalin … In Poland, too, tragic events occurred when innocent people were sent to
15 their death. Many others were imprisoned, often for many years, although innocent, including Communists … We have put an end to this system, or we are putting an end to it once and for all.

Although he had to tread carefully, given recent Soviet intervention in Hungary, Gomulka did succeed in relaxing the Soviet stranglehold over Poland, symbolised by the return home of thousands of Soviet officers who had been serving with the Polish Army.

Gomulka's words and actions were not those of a servile Soviet puppet. Moscow tolerated Gomulka because he succeeded in keeping the Communists in power. But he insisted that any Soviet troop movements on Polish soil should first be approved by the Poles. In 1970 Gomulka was to achieve a notable diplomatic success: West German recognition of Poland's Oder-Neisse frontier, imposed on Germany at the end of the War. Gomulka's failure was due ultimately to lack of a long-term strategy and his inability, repeated by other Eastern Bloc leaders, to win the population over to Communism. Gomulka spent more time on manoeuvring between different factions in the Party than on tackling economic and administrative problems. He became less flexible and more disillusioned as problems grew, and he became a scapegoat for economic problems such as declining production. In December 1970 the Government announced an increase in food prices of 30 per cent. The predictable demonstrations and clashes between workers and police followed. Gomulka was removed by the Central Committee.

2 Gierek and Poland

> **KEY ISSUE** How successful were Gierek's policies inside Poland?

Gomulka's successor Edward Gierek reversed the price increases but also favoured a longer-term solution to economic problems. He wanted to rely less on the USSR and create more financial and economic links with the West. He talked of reform and decentralisation, brought more experts into the administration, and put less emphasis on ideological correctness and more on practical solutions.

BIOGRAPHY: EDWARD GIEREK (1913-)

Gierek spent his youth in France, became a miner and joined the French Communist Party in 1931. During the Second World War he fought in the French and Belgian resistance. Back in Poland, Gierek became a mining union organiser in Silesia, later promoting many old friends from that region. Gierek formed the Polish Workers' Party in 1945 and joined the Politburo in 1956. His reputation was initially as an effective administrator. However, like Gomulka before him, his management created the impression that ultimately the Communists could not guarantee material prosperity for the Polish people, and he paid the price after a long spell as First Secretary of the Polish Workers' Party between 1970 and 1980.

However, he caused offence by his apparent servility to the USSR: in 1976 cooperation between Poland and the USSR was officially strengthened, and in 1979 he gave unconditional backing to the Soviet invasion of Afghanistan. Gierek was ultimately brought down by events in 1980: more price rises, strikes and the rise of *Solidarity* (see chapter 6).

3 Imre Nagy and Hungary

> **KEY ISSUE** What were the main features of Nagy's policies inside Hungary and why were they controversial?

Imre Nagy in Hungary was an example of a Communist reformer who was considered dangerously radical and who suffered from the political maneouvrings which followed in the wake of Khrushchev's destalinisation after Stalin's death in 1953. Nagy wanted to increase support for the Communists among the working class. The Hungarian People's Independence Front, established in 1949, comprised several parties, including Communists and Socialists. Nagy acknowledged that the Front was little more than a rubber stamp for decisions made

---

BIOGRAPHY: IMRE NAGY (1896-1956)

Like most Communist leaders of this era, Nagy underwent a long and difficult political apprenticeship after humble beginnings. He was taken prisoner in Russia during the First World War, and in 1918 he joined the Hungarian section of the Russian Communist Party. On his return to Hungary in 1921 he joined the Socialists, because the Communists were banned. Nagy had a spell in prison, then spent a long period in Russia, becoming a collective farm director in 1937. Later in Hungary he opposed rapid collectivisation and favoured economic reforms which were quite liberal by Stalinist standards. Significantly, Nagy was friendly with Malenkov, who implemented a 'New Course' in the Soviet economy after Stalin's death, putting more emphasis on the consumers' needs for everyday goods.

Nagy was rapidly promoted in postwar Hungary. He was appointed Minister of the Interior and President of the National Assembly. However, after opposition from Rákosi, he was expelled from the Politburo in 1949. Then in 1953 the post-Stalin Soviet Government, keen to avert popular discontent and wanting changes in Hungary, foisted Nagy on to the Hungarian Government at the expense of Rákosi, and he was free to implement his New Course. There followed the trauma of the Hungarian Rising. Following its suppression, Nagy was executed by the Soviets. He was posthumously rehabilitated in 1989.

by the Communist leadership. He therefore proposed a Patriotic People's Front, to be a democratic and popular organisation. Members would be allowed to set up their own local branches and non-Party members would be encouraged to join in political debate.

Nagy's aim was similar to that of Gorbachev in the USSR many years later, and he was as naive as the Soviet leader in assuming that the Communist Party could retain a leading and popular role in such a democratic system. Reformers like Nagy were both optimistic and naive because, as Communists, they had been schooled for years in a doctrine which made it impossible for them to contemplate their Party not being successful in the long run. Nagy's more hardline opponents like Rákosi opposed the Patriotic People's Front, and Nagy was attacked within the Party for 'rightist deviation'. During 1955 he was progressively expelled from the Politburo, the Central Committee and the Party itself. It was a fate which befell other reforming Communists who tried to change the system from within.

4 Kádár and Hungary

> **KEY ISSUE** What were the main features of Kádár's regime inside Hungary and why did his regime last for so long?

After the Hungarian Rising, the new leader János Kádár proved a more orthodox Communist in his approach. He did not repudiate all reform on principle, and indeed was in power when the New Economic Mechanism was implemented. Nevertheless, Kádár was firmly against a multi-party regime and any notion of leaving the Warsaw Pact. Like other Communist leaders, he expelled his opponents, including Rákosi, from the Party. Kádár was to prove one of the longest serving leaders in the Eastern Bloc. However, like others in his position such as Zhivkov in Bulgaria and Honecker in the GDR, whilst guiding his country through several political and economic developments, as a representative of the old order he ultimately proved inflexible and fell victim to the fundamental changes of direction of the late 1980s.

In the 1960s Kádár was flexible and felt secure enough to relax some aspects of the authoritarian regime. He made the very unStalinist-like declaration: 'Whereas the Rákosites used to say that those who are not with us are against us, we say, those who are not against us are with us.' In other words, provided that the people accepted the constraints of single-party rule and showed at least outward conformity, there would not be harsh repression and the population could expect rising living standards.

Kádár made concessions: rehabilitation for purge victims and survivors of the 1956 Rising, a relaxation of censorship of foreign books and films, more opportunities in higher education, and an

---

BIOGRAPHY: JÁNOS KÁDÁR (1912-89)

Kádár was born to a peasant family in Fiume in 1912, but was taken by his mother to Budapest. He trained as a mechanic and joined the illegal Hungarian Communist Party in 1931. He spent two years in prison, and then from 1940 he fought in the resistance and helped to reconstruct the Hungarian Communist Party. He was arrested by the Germans. After the War he was elected to the Politburo, becoming Minister of Internal Affairs in 1948. He was arrested in 1951 on charges of anti-Stalinism. He was rehabilitated in 1954 and joined Nagy's Government in October 1956, proclaiming that 'the Communist Party had degenerated into perpetuating despotism and national slavery.' But Kádár feared that Nagy was going too far and disassociated himself from reform just in time. After the Rising he was chosen by the Soviets as Nagy's replacement. He was at various times First Secretary and Prime Minister. Although regarded by many Hungarians as a traitor because of his support for Soviet intervention, Kádár modified his severity in the 1960s. However, he always supported the USSR and resisted reform in the 1980s, although the Hungarian emigré writer George Mikes wrote in 1986 that 'It is his inclination to decency, his respect for Hungary's western traditions and the comparative economic well-being he created that made Communism almost popular in Hungary.' Kádár was sacked in 1989.

---

agreement with the Vatican over the appointment of bishops. Kádár was able to survive the fall of his mentor Khrushchev and the deaths of later Soviet leaders. By reducing the dependence of Hungary on the USSR he won respect abroad and enough popularity inside Hungary for there to be an increase in Communist Party membership. He also avoided the excesses of the personality cult that developed in some Eastern Bloc states. Greater stability brought limited political change: in 1966 contested elections were allowed in Hungary, albeit between 'approved' candidates, in place of the single Party list.

However, many professionals and intellectuals took advantage of the new freedoms to leave Hungary, and reformers believed that economic reform must be accompanied by political reform if further progress were to be made. Multi-candidate elections became compulsory from 1983, and in 1985 some independent candidates were voted into parliament, defeating some prominent Party representatives. However, Kádár was only prepared to countenance change within prescribed limits. Those who were too vocal in their criticism of the regime still courted trouble. Although Kádár tried to occupy the middle ground, he was increasingly seen as rigid in approach by a new generation, which included younger members of the Party and which was concerned at the failure of the Hungarian economic experiment. These Hungarians concluded that the existing regime could not deliver its promise of being able to consistently raise the living standards of the people. Ultimately even Kádár fell victim to a mood favouring political pluralism rather than a one-party authoritarian state.

5 Husák and Czechoslovakia

> **KEY ISSUE** To what extent did Husák succeed in restoring 'normality' to Czechoslovakia following the 1968 crisis?

There were parallels between Kádár's career and that of Gustav Husák, who dominated Czechoslovak politics after the suppression of the reform movement of 1968 and Dubček's dismissal (see chapter 6) until his own fall from power in 1989. Husák too tried to steer a middle course between reformers and hardliners. However, critics accused Husák of seeking personal popularity, and he was less successful than Kádár in maintaining support for the Party: after 1968 there was a general air of apathy in the Czechoslovak Communist Party. Membership remained substantial only because it was necessary for career advancement. The Party's own reports revealed that active Party work at the local level had virtually ceased. Since the USSR insisted upon conformity and compliance, the response of many citizens was to opt out of political life. Husák was compelled to employ sustained propaganda, periodic purges and a generally hardline stance in order to maintain Party control, and the Czech Government, along with the East German and Romanian ones, held out longest against significant change in the late 1980s.

BIOGRAPHY: GUSTAV HUSÁK (1913-91)

Husák, from a middle-class Bratislava family, joined the Communists in 1934. He practised as a lawyer between 1938 and 1942, then played a prominent part in the Slovak resistance. After the War he was a victim of the purges: he was sentenced in 1954 to life imprisonment for 'Slovak bourgeois nationalism'. Released in 1960, he became a construction worker, was forgiven his 'crimes', and rejoined the Party in 1963. Although part of its reformist wing, he abandoned it just as Soviet intervention was threatened in 1968 and therefore narrowly survived the crisis. Afterwards he was appointed First Secretary, and in 1975 also became Head of State. He became one of the leading spokesmen of the Warsaw Pact. Husák fell from power in 1989 and was expelled from the Communist Party in February 1990.

---

6 Ulbricht, the GDR and the Berlin Wall

> **KEY ISSUE** How successful were Ulbricht's hardline policies within the GDR?

The East German leaders Walter Ulbricht and Eric Honecker fitted the Western image of the grey, inflexible, hardline Communist leader better than some of their counterparts in the Eastern Bloc. Partly this was a question of personality, and partly a reflection of the peculiar position of the GDR, regarded in many quarters as an artificial creation and unsure for a long time of its long-term future. Nevertheless the leaders were far more than docile puppets of Moscow. Under Ulbricht, who became the SED leader in 1950 and played an important role in setting up the new state, the GDR became, by Eastern Bloc standards, a relatively cohesive and prosperous state.

> **BIOGRAPHY: WALTER ULBRICHT (1893-1973)**
> Ulbricht was born in Leipzig, the son of a tailor. He was apprenticed as a carpenter and joined the Marxist Spartacist League before the First World War. Afterwards he spent several years in the USSR. He became a Communist deputy in the German parliament in 1928, then after Hitler's accession to power lived in France and the USSR. He fought in the Spanish Civil War and was charged with eliminating anti-Stalinists on the Left. He was in Moscow during the Second World War and was one of the founders of the Socialist Unity Party. Ulbricht had good Stalinist credentials, led the GDR for over 20 years, and as Party leader, Chairman of the Council of State and Head of the Armed Forces, he combined Party and state leadership until his removal in 1971.

Some of Ulbricht's colleagues disliked his intransigence and cult of personality, and blamed him for the disturbances of 1953 outlined in Chapter 6. However, as a skilled operator he removed his political opponents within the Party. The GDR never experienced mass discontent again until the late 1980s. Although it faced economic pressures, particularly when compared with West Germany, the World Bank placed the GDR's economy twelfth in the world ranking in 1984, and it had the highest standard of living of any socialist state.

The destalinisation of the mid and late 1950s had little impact on the GDR. Ulbricht's own disavowal of Stalinism, required by the new Soviet leadership, was lukewarm, and those advocating reform were harassed or imprisoned. Much of Ulbricht's attention was focused on the status and geography of Berlin. Thousands of the GDR's citizens used West Berlin as an escape route to the West, with its promise of personal freedom and a better material standard of living. The exodus was a drain on the economy, since most of the refugees were from the younger generation. It was also a political embarrassment to the regime. In 1953 alone over 300,000 East German workers emigrated to the West. After a fall in numbers, the exodus increased again in 1960. To counter the exodus, Ulbricht personally pressed for the building of the Berlin Wall, which was done on 13 August 1961 to prevent access to West Berlin. Ulbricht believed that the GDR must be totally separated from the West if Socialism were to be built at home. Behind the Wall he hoped to create a modern industrialised state.

The Warsaw Pact issued a communiqué on the same day that the wall was built:

1 The Governments of the Warsaw Treaty member states have been striving for a peaceful settlement with Germany for a number of years … the Governments of the Western Powers have not so far shown willingness to achieve an agreed solution of this question through negotia-
5 tions between all sides concerned. Moreover, to the peaceful proposals of the Socialist countries, the Western powers reply by stepping up their military preparations, fanning up war hysteria and by threatening to use armed forces … The Governments of the Western Powers, in every way encouraging the arming of Western Germany, grossly violate the most
10 important international agreements envisaging eradication of German militarism and preventing its revival in any form … subversive centres are smuggling their agents to the GDR for all sorts of subversion, recruiting spies and inciting hostile elements to organise sabotage and to provoke disturbances in the GDR … The Government bodies and
15 military concerns of the Federal Republic, through deceit, bribery, and blackmail, make some unstable elements in the GDR leave for Western Germany …

The Governments of the Warsaw Treaty member states address the GDR … with a proposal to establish such an order on the borders of
20 West Berlin which would securely block the way for the subversive activity against the Socialist camp countries … At the same time, the Governments of the Warsaw Treaty member states find it necessary to emphasise that this necessity will disappear when a peaceful settlement with Germany is achieved.

The GDR Government published its own decree:

1 The interests of preserving peace demand that an end be put to the machinations of the West German revanchists and militarists and that the way be opened, through conclusion of a German peace treaty, to the preservation of peace and the revival of Germany as a peaceful, anti-
5 imperialist, neutral state. The viewpoint of the Bonn Government that World War II is not yet formally ended is tantamount to demanding freedom for militarist provocations and civil war measures.

This imperialist policy, which is being carried out under the signboard of anti-communism, constitutes continuation of the aggressive aims of
10 the Fascist German imperialism of the time of the Third Reich … The

Adenauer Government is systematically carrying out, with regard to the German Democratic Republic, preparations for a civil war ... The West German revanchists and militarists are abusing the peaceful policy of the USSR and the Warsaw Treaty states on the German question, in order
15 to damage not only the German Democratic Republic but also other states of the Socialist camp by means of rampant, hostile propaganda, by enticing people and by sabotage ...

Reliable safeguards and effective control must be ensured on the West Berlin borders in order to block the way of subversive activities ...
20 This decree ... remains valid until the conclusion of a German peace treaty.

The Berlin Wall became the ultimate symbol of both the physical and ideological barriers dividing East and West Europe during the Cold War. It succeeded in keeping in the East German population and was probably Ulbricht's most enduring legacy, along with recognition of the GDR's existence as a state in its own right. Ulbricht fought to achieve this throughout the 1950s and 1960s, and would not establish diplomatic relations with the West Germans until they recognised the sovereign status of the GDR. Meanwhile, other than a brief period of relaxation in the early 1960s when writers and artists were allowed to criticise the excesses of Stalinism and West Germans were allowed to visit the East, a hard line was enforced. Intellectuals who urged a more 'humane socialism' were usually arrested in Ulbricht's GDR.

Ulbricht did not always get his way. He was at odds with the USSR over its attempts to do a deal with West Germany. Ulbricht was forced to endorse the treaty between the USSR and West Germany in 1970 confirming Germany's postwar borders. However, his opposition led to his replacement as First Secretary in May 1971 by Erich Honecker.

7 Honecker and the GDR

> **KEY ISSUE** What were the main features of Honecker's regime inside the GDR?

Honecker, like Ulbricht, was a hardliner. He had led the clampdown on reformist ideas after the Czechoslovakian crisis in 1968 and continued to react strongly against expressions of dissent at home. However, he was more pragmatic in his foreign policy, which he brought more into line with the Soviet policy of *détente*, or a relaxation of Cold War tensions. Whereas the leadership's stated objective had been a reunified Germany under socialist leadership, the goal was now the more realistic one of *Abgrenzung* or 'separate development'. In 1974 the GDR changed from the 'socialist state of the German nation' into the more modest 'socialist state of workers and peasants'. Honecker's commitment to *détente* paid off. In 1971 a Four-Power

---

BIOGRAPHY: ERICH HONECKER (1912-94)

Honecker was born in the Saarland to a mining family. He joined the German Communist Party in 1929 and spent many of the years between 1935 and 1945 in a Nazi prison. In the East German state he was given responsibility for Central Committee authority over security from 1956, and was groomed by Ulbricht for the succession. Always loyal to Ulbricht, Honecker was entrusted with difficult tasks such as the building of the Berlin Wall. He was also an expert on Party organisation and administration. Having succeeded Ulbricht as First Secretary in 1971, Honecker became Head of State in 1976, and was ousted from power in 1989. After accusations of abuse of power, he was given sanctuary in the former USSR.

Agreement on Berlin reaffirmed the special status of Berlin and new trade and travel arrangements between West Germany and Berlin. In 1972 the two Germanies recognised each other's sovereignty and equal status, and in 1973 both joined the United Nations as separate states. Soon afterwards 68 nations recognised the sovereign status of the GDR. Although Soviet caution put a brake on further attempts by Honecker to improve relations with West Germany, he caused a surprise during a visit to West Germany in 1987 by expressing his hope for a united Germany. Honecker faced a dilemma: for a generation the West Germans had been portrayed in the East not only as 'brother Germans' but as potential enemies in league with capitalist great powers. But his achievements were welcome to many ordinary Germans, because they facilitated contacts between divided German families. The regime also made some social progress, for example increasing social benefits. Citizens were encouraged to take pride in national sporting achievements. However, ultimately Honecker could not disguise the disparity in wealth between East and West Germany. The Party's élite was increasingly enmeshed in its own incompetence and corruption, and Honecker himself acquired an island in the Baltic. Like other long-serving Communist leaders, he appeared increasingly inflexible, out-of-touch and unable to comprehend the popular wave of dissent which swept across the Eastern Bloc in the late 1980s.

8 Gheorghiu-Dej, Ceaușescu and Romania

KEY ISSUE What were the principal features of the Communist regime inside Romania?

Other Eastern Bloc leaders had distinctive characteristics of their own. In Romania Gheorghiu-Dej was Party leader and from 1961 until his death in 1965 also President. Although a close ally of Stalin and then Khrushchev, it was under his leadership that Romania began to adopt a position of semi-independence in the Eastern Bloc. During the Hungarian Rising he declared the 'inadvisability of foreign intervention in the affairs of other countries' and gave temporary refuge to the deposed Imre Nagy. Yet he also approved of the suppression of the Rising, not least because Romania's own ethnic Hungarian population expressed its sympathies with the rebels! Later Gheorghiu-Dej established closer relations with China, Albania and Yugoslavia, all at loggerheads with the USSR. He defied Soviet pressure to run Romania as a granary supplying food to the Eastern Bloc and industrialised Romania during the 1950s and 1960s. A campaign of 'Romanianisation' emphasised national traditions and rejected Russian influence. The regime refused to participate in Warsaw Pact exercises. The Party published a declaration in 1964:

1 The world communist movement and the socialist camp are now faced with a split ... The victories of the Romanian People's Republic and the other socialist countries show that the successful solution of the tasks of developing the economy depends first and foremost on the utilisation
5 of each country's internal possibilities through an intense mustering of its own forces and the maximum use of natural resources.
   Decisive for the development of the countries which inherited economic backwardness from capitalism is socialist industrialisation ...
   The idea of a single planning body for all COMECON countries has
10 the most serious economic and political implications. The planned management of the national economy is one of the fundamental, essential and inalienable attributes of the sovereignty of the socialist state ...
   Beginning with the Leninist truth according to which the states and national distinctions will be maintained until the victory of socialism on
15 a world plane, and even a long time after, the socialist countries can achieve their unity of action in all domains, economic as well as political, by reciprocal consultation ... and not by establishing exclusive solutions by some superstate authority ...
   Bearing in mind the diversity of the conditions of socialist construc-
20 tion, there are not and there can be no unique patterns and recipes; no one can decide what is and what is not correct for other countries or parties ...
   It is the exclusive right of each party to independently work out its political line, its concrete objectives and the ways and means of attaining
25 them ... No party has or can have a privileged place, or can impose its line or opinions on other parties ...
   Let all of us unite to bar the road to a split, to safeguard the unity and cohesion of the countries of the socialist camp, the world communist and working class movement.

The USSR tolerated this independent approach partly because Romania was a small, relatively undeveloped state, and was not considered much of a threat. Probably more important was the fact

BIOGRAPHY: NICOLAE CEAUŞESCU (1918-89)
Ceauşescu was born into a peasant family and worked in a Bucharest factory from the age of 11. He joined the Romanian Communist Party in 1936. After several spells in prison he rose rapidly through the Party, becoming its leader in 1965 and Head of State in 1967. He was the youngest Eastern Bloc leader at the time of his accession. Ceauşescu's policies of forced economic development, conformity and an exaggerated personality cult eventually provoked a reaction. Following the 'Winter Revolution' of December 1989, Ceauşescu and his wife were executed.

that the Romanian state remained socialist in its essence. The Romanians preached National Communism rather than the Soviet brand of international socialist brotherhood. Nevertheless, they were not about to introduce capitalist or liberal deviations into their structures. That *would* have led to fears of counter-revolution, as surfaced in the crises involving Hungary and Czechoslovakia. Romania signed a Treaty of Friendship and Mutual Aid with Moscow in 1970, and a fundamental break in relations was averted.

Nicolae Ceauşescu continued Gheorghiu-Dej's policies of strict control at home and an independent stance within the Eastern Bloc. He fostered relations with China and initiated joint economic projects

A pro-Ceauşescu parade in Romania in 1969

with Yugoslavia. In 1967 Romania became the first Eastern Bloc country to establish diplomatic relations with West Germany; in 1968 it condemned the invasion of Czechoslovakia; and continued to limit its participation in both COMECON and the Warsaw Pact. Ceauşescu was distinctive in his personal style of ruling and elevated the cult of personality to heights unknown elsewhere in the Eastern Bloc. In addition to holding several Party and state positions himself, Ceauşescu promoted his family. His wife Elena was both powerful and feared, being more ambitious, intelligent and charismatic than her husband. By the late 1970s four members of Ceauşescu's family were on the Party Central Committee. By 1989 50 members of the family held important posts in the Party or Government. Ceauşescu treated Romania like a personal fiefdom, building opulent palaces whilst life for the people became ever harder.

Despite Romania's weak power base, Ceauşescu was assiduously courted by the West. His independent stance offered the prospect of a chink in the Iron Curtain to exploit. The future American President George Bush described Ceauşescu in 1983 as 'one of Europe's good Communists'. In 1978 the Ceauşescus were given a state visit to Britain and were entertained by the Queen. Ceauşescu used these contacts to join organisations like the International Monetary Fund and the World Bank, and got preferential trading status with the European Community. None of this benefited ordinary Romanians. The introduction of multi-candidate elections to parliament in 1974 simply masked the steadily increasing power of the Party and Ceauşescu's own dictatorship. Other national groups suffered most: in particular the 1.6 million Hungarians within Romania suffered a programme of 'Romanianisation' in an attempt to dilute their separate identity. The autonomous Hungarian region suffered the lowest level of economic development in Romania.

9 Zhivkov and Bulgaria

> **KEY ISSUE** Why was Zhivkov's regime inside Bulgaria so long-lasting?

Todor Zhivkov dominated Bulgaria between 1954 and his fall from power in 1989, partly because he was an astute politician, ruthless or conciliatory as the occasion demanded. He purged opponents, then instituted reforms. Although sometimes criticised within Bulgaria for subservience towards Moscow, Zhivkov's strength was partly due to the fact that he did cultivate Soviet support. However, his success was also due to his eradication of domestic opposition, his firm control of domestic and foreign policy, and the fact that for a long time many of his economic policies were successful. The intelligentsia toed the Party line, and even the Bulgarian Church gave its blessing to the regime,

---

BIOGRAPHY: TODOR ZHIVKOV (1911-98)

Born into a poor peasant family, Zhivkov later joined the Communists and had a good record of resistance to the Nazis during the Second World War. In 1945 he was commander of the militia, arresting thousands of opponents of the Communists. He became First Secretary following Khrushchev's 'Secret Speech' of 1956 against Stalinism. Zhivkov survived Khrushchev's fall in 1964, switching his support to Brezhnev at the opportune moment. He defeated a plot against himself by prominent figures in the Party and Army and went on to be President and even Prime Minister. He was jailed for corruption in 1992, and eventually released from house arrest in 1997. Zhivkov's distinction was to be the Eastern Bloc's longest-serving leader.

---

declaring in 1967 that 'the great majority of the people have already freed themselves from the shackles of religion and religious morality.'

Zhivkov demonstrated his loyalty to the Soviets by participating in the invasion of Czechoslovakia and supporting Brezhnev's policy on *détente*. Zhivkov declared in 1962 that the Bulgarian 'political watch is exact to the second with the watch of the Soviet Union ... Our watch is working towards Moscow time. This is a matter of great pride for all Bulgarian people.' Zhivkov frequently acted as a channel for diplomatic contacts between the USSR and the West, since he inspired trust abroad.

At home the picture was less rosy. Bulgarian relations with Yugoslavia and Greece were sometimes soured by Bulgarian claims to Yugoslavia's Macedonian population. Bulgaria itself contained a large Turkish population. The regime pressured thousands of Turks to emigrate from Southern Dobrudja, which Bulgaria acquired in 1940. Then in 1984 the Government began a campaign to assimilate the Turkish minority, restricting the use of the Turkish language. The concept of a Bulgarian national culture was promoted, although it did not have the anti-Soviet edge which distinguished Romanian nationalism.

Zhivkov's image became tarnished in the 1980s. There were allegations of Bulgarian involvement in the attempted assassination of the Pope in 1981. His attempt to divert attention from economic problems by stepping up the campaign against the Turkish minority carried little credibility. As with other other Eastern Bloc leaders, as economic problems became more pronounced and he himself seemed inflexible, so the pressure for radical change became stronger and stronger, and Zhivkov responded with too little and too late.

10 Assessment

> **KEY ISSUE** Why were the long-established Communist regimes of the Eastern Bloc unable to retain power in the 1980s?

Whatever the achievements in retaining power for so long and dealing with potentially difficult situations such as reconciling national interests with the need to keep on good terms with their Soviet mentor, none of the Eastern Bloc leaders in power during the 1980s was able to retain his position once the buttress of Soviet support began to crumble. Movements for radical reform were becoming more confident. Ultimately, ordinary people were no longer prepared to passively accept the economic, social and political system which they and their parents had endured for two generations. Once the new Soviet leader Mikhail Gorbachev began his own campaign for reform in 1985, the Eastern Bloc leaders came under pressure to do the same.

Making notes on 'Leadership and Politics in the Eastern Bloc'

In compiling your notes, concentrate on acquiring knowledge and understanding of the contributions which each of the Eastern Bloc leaders and their regimes in this chapter made towards the nature of Communist rule in their countries. How important was their leadership? Were there similarities and differences in their policies? How did the regimes maintain themselves in power? Were they successful in the short and long terms? By what criteria do we judge success? What significant events took place in the history of the Eastern Bloc countries between the early 1950s and the mid 1980s (the crises in Hungary, Czechoslovakia and Poland are dealt with in Chapter 6)?

Essay questions on Chapters 3 and 4

The material from chapters 3 and 4 will be useful when tackling essays on individual countries during this period, or questions which invite a comparison between two or more states. Questions may well focus on why the Communist regimes managed to stay in power for so long or the significance of particular leaders. It may be necessary in some cases to include material from Chapters 5 and 6.

The following essays are typical of what might be expected:

1. a) Outline the main events in the history of the GDR (East Germany) between 1949 and the breaching of the Berlin Wall in 1989;

   b) How far do you agree with the statement that 'The most remarkable fact about the GDR was that, for an artificial creation, it lasted so long'?

2. With reference to any TWO of the following countries, explain

why the Communist regimes succeeded in retaining power for so
long after 1949: Poland; Czechoslovakia; Hungary; Bulgaria; Romania.
3. a) Outline the main policies of any TWO of the following: Gomulka;
Ulbricht; Zhivkov; Ceauşescu;
b) What was the significance of the period of office of your two
choices for the history of their countries?

In Question 1a), the key word is 'Outline': all you are required to do is
briefly describe the most notable events in the history of the GDR
during this period, including topics such as the building of the Berlin
Wall, economic reform, and the policies of its leaders. The key words
in part b) are 'How far do you agree', 'remarkable fact', 'artificial
creation' and 'lasted so long.' The key theme is the fact that the GDR
survived as a separate state for over 40 years, although its existence
was in doubt for some time. Do not get too bogged down in detail, but
adopt an analytical approach. Whether you agree that the regime's
survival was the most remarkable fact about it, rather than, say, its
economic development, is a matter of judgement. However, you
should deal with the concept of 'artificiality'. For many years after
1945 it was not certain that a separate state *would* be created or even
sponsored by the USSR. You might also consider the difficulties which
the regime had in establishing acceptance of its sovereignty by the
outside world, and to affirm the reality and not just the image of a
separate identity. The very fact of the building of the Berlin Wall might
be taken as evidence of a lack of confidence by the regime in its own
citizens. However, you might also consider some of the achievements
of the regime: it *did* eventually win acceptance by the international
community; and despite problems, its economy performed well in
comparison to some Communist states. If you can convey perspective
by briefly referring to some developments in neighbouring states, so
much the better.

The key words in essay 2 are 'reference to any TWO', 'explain why'
and 'succeeded in retaining power for so long.' The theme is clear
enough: although Communist regimes were overturned at the end of
the 1980s, they had all managed to remain in power for several
decades. Why was this? The question is not asking for an analysis of
why and *how* the Communist regimes came to power, although the
methods used by the Communists to defeat their opponents, and the
use of Soviet influence, were in evidence after 1949 as well as before.
Factors to be considered include: the role of the USSR; the tactics of
propaganda, manipulation and intimidation employed by one-party
authoritarian regimes; and economic progress, at least initially. When
Communist regimes were seriously threatened, or Communist
reformers themselves proposed radical policies, there was the threat of
outside intervention. To what extent did the regimes have any popular
backing, and to what extent were they dictatorial regimes, sustained
ultimately by force? The important point as ever is that you should

argue a case, with appropriate supporting evidence.

For part (a) of essay 3 you should briefly outline the main policies of the two leaders of your choice. The key word in part (b) is 'significance', and you are being asked to analyse the importance or significance of the chosen individuals in their countries in the short and long term. Whilst supporting your arguments with evidence, the focus of the answer should be: what was the leaders' role? Did they succeed in carrying out their aims? What were those aims? Did they affect that country's development? For example, Gomulka's importance in Poland centred on two periods. First, after the War, he helped to establish a Communist Government. However, at the same time he succeeded to some extent in following an independent line from Stalin, so that Poland did not follow the Soviet model entirely, for example in agricultural policy. In the second period Gomulka was back in power between 1956 and 1970. During this time he kept the Communists in control but failed to resolve Poland's economic problems, and he paid the price when domestic unrest became serious - setting the pattern for later crises which saw the emergence of *Solidarity*. As always with this type of question, do not be afraid to express a firm opinion about issues of significance, as long as you can produce enough evidence to make a credible argument.

Source-based questions on 'Leaderhip and Politics in the Eastern Bloc'

1. *Gomulka's speech after the 1956 crisis in Poland*
Read Gomulka's speech on page 42. Answer the following questions:

a) Using your own knowledge, explain what had caused the 'workers of Poznan' to demonstrate in 1956, and why this had caused a crisis for the Communist regime. (5 marks)
b) Summarise Gomulka's explanation of the crisis. How accurate was it? (6 marks)
c) Comment on the tone of Gomulka's speech. (4 marks)
d) To what extent did Gomulka succeed in 'putting an end to the system'? (5 marks)

2. *The building of the Berlin Wall, 1961*
Read carefully the extracts from the Warsaw Pact Communiqué and the GDR Council of Ministers' decree on pages 49-50. Answer the following questions:

a) Using your own knowledge, outline the events which led to the building of the Berlin Wall in 1961. (3 marks)
b) Compare the reasons given in the two sources to justify the building of the Wall. (6 marks)
c) Comment on the use of propaganda in both sources. (6 marks)
d) To what extent did the Berlin Wall fulfil the aims of the East German regime in building it? (5 marks)

3. National Communism in Romania

Read the extract from the Romanian Workers' Party declaration on page 52. Answer the following questions:

a) Using your own knowledge, explain what had happened in relation to COMECON to prompt this declaration. (3 marks)

b) What arguments are used in the declaration to justify the Romanian Party following its own line? (5 marks)

c) What was there in this statement to concern Soviet and other Eastern Bloc leaders? (4 marks)

d) How skilful is the use of propaganda to make the authors' case? (4 marks)

e) Using your own knowledge, outline the extent to which the Romanian regime succeeded in implementing these principles before 1989. (4 marks)

Summary Diagram

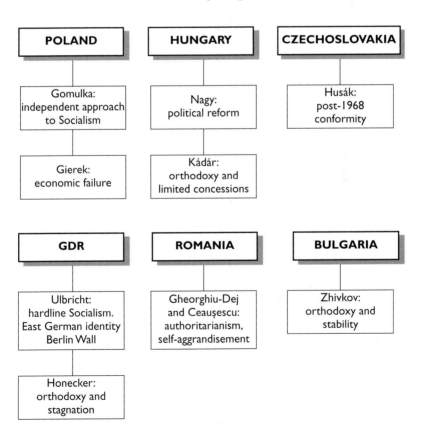

5 Economic Systems

POINTS TO CONSIDER

This chapter will introduce you to the main economic systems and policies followed by the various Communist regimes of Poland, Czechoslovakia, Hungary, East Germany, Romania and Bulgaria during the three decades following the establishment of Communist rule in the late 1940s. Your aim on first reading the chapter should be to understand the basic principles of the Stalinist economic structures established in the various states, the extent to which they were similar to, or different from, each other, the extent to which they were adapted during the period covered by this book, and the extent to which the economic systems were effective.

1 Stalinist Politics and Economics

KEY ISSUE What were the principal features of the Stalinist command economy, and what were its successes and failures?

Long before the Second World War Stalin's USSR had exhibited characteristics which strongly influenced the postwar Communist regimes of Eastern and Central Europe, although there were differences as well as similarities between them. Politically Stalinism meant a one-party state, in which political control was marked by authoritarianism and propaganda designed to enforce support or at least compliance. It meant the total politicisation of life, so that the citizen's thoughts as well as actions were dictated by the state. Economically, the Stalinist state was characterised by a highly centralised economic system, which involved central planning and priority for heavy industry. The economy responded to the priorities set by the regime and not to consumer demand. The Stalinist state was conservative: despite the original revolutionary ethos of Marxism, the development of a Party hierarchy with entrenched privilege and large unwieldy bureaucracies worked against change. Too many people had a stake in the existing way of doing things to have an incentive for change, even when individuals recognised the need for radical measures.

It was scarcely surprising that the essentials of the Stalinist 'system' were adopted by the Eastern Bloc regimes. Most of the Eastern Bloc leaders had come through a long and difficult apprenticeship before achieving power in their own countries. They believed in the Stalinist system and had often suffered persecution for it. Also the Kremlin expected conformity. The Soviet way was the one way to Socialism. Any major attempt to change the system threatened the Communist monopoly of power as well as the orthodox ideology - and tolerating change in one country might encourage it elsewhere. Also, it was evident that in certain respects the Stalinist way of doing things actually worked. For all its faults, the Stalinist model had proved a brutal but effective way of building a heavy industrial base very quickly in a peasant-based economy, and boosting quantity if not quality. Likewise, although collectivisation of agriculture had been unpopular with the peasants and had not markedly increased output, it had secured food supplies for the state and had given the Party a hold over the countryside.

The Marxist vision of a Socialist utopia assumed a developed industrial base, and in this respect much of the Eastern and Central European region was deficient. Certainly, compared with Western Europe, the region was short on basic raw materials like fossil fuels and iron ore, with exceptions such as the Romanian oil fields. Some areas were more developed industrially. It was not certain that the Stalinist economic model would benefit more mature economies such as those of East Germany and the Czech lands, but in the aftermath of the War little thought was given to this.

Not everything imposed by Communist regimes after coming to power was done against the wishes of the local population. Most of the regimes of prewar Eastern Europe had been narrowly based and reactionary in their social and economic policies. There had been marked differences within societies, particularly between town and countryside. This was particularly noticeable for example in Hungary, where there had been a division between the more liberal, Westernised urban culture and the conservative, nationalist and anti-Semitic peasantry. Ethnic divisions had frequently produced intolerance and strong political infighting. After 1945 there was a popular mood for change and optimism for the future. The Stalinist model appeared to offer advantages to many people: for example, a basic level of social security and employment to all who conformed. To those without a history of democratic rights, trading a personal freedom they had never had for the basics of life did not necessarily present the same difficulty of choice it would have done for a citizen brought up in liberal Western Europe. Only when it became clear that the Communist regimes could not deliver the promised economic goods did the implicit social contract between rulers and ruled begin to break down, notably in the 1980s.

Although Stalin died in 1953, his social and economic 'system' lasted in essence long after his death. Subsequent reformers like Khrushchev were prepared to make adaptations but not destroy the basics of the one-party state or command economy. Only with Gorbachev in the 1980s was there a leader prepared to make fundamental reforms, and even he assumed initially that the Party would remain in control of the process. By then the Communist regimes within the Soviet Bloc were already experiencing serious crises of their own.

2 Agriculture in the Eastern Bloc

KEY ISSUE What were the principal features of agricultural organisation in the countries of the Eastern Bloc, and how successful were agricultural policies?

The Stalinist approach to agriculture had involved reorganising small peasant farms into large collectives. This was adopted as an ideal in all the Eastern Bloc states except Poland, although there were some variations in agricultural practice between the different states and experiments to increase production. Under the Soviet model, peasants on collectivised farms worked on a cooperative basis, although they were allowed small private plots on which they could farm for themselves. The farms had to meet a quota determined by the state, which also decided on a set price; then other debts and expenses would be paid off. Any remaining profit could then be shared by members of the collective.

The percentage of collectivised land, or land on state farms, in some Eastern Bloc economies

	1952	1953	1954	1955	1956	1957	1958
Czechoslovakia	43	43	42	43	49	68	87
GDR	3*	30	28	33	30	34	90
Hungary	37	39	31	34	39	12*	77
Poland	17	19	19	24	22	13	13

(* percentage under collective ownership)

(Source: (ed.) M.C. Kaser, *The Economic History of Eastern Europe*, Volume 3, Oxford 1986.)

In Hungary large landowners had their land confiscated by the state in 1945. However, the unpopularity of collectivisation was recognised by Imre Nagy: under his 'New Course', he was prepared to allow peasants to leave the farms. Following the Hungarian Rising, Kádár in 1959 began a three year process of reimposing collectivisation, although under the New Economic Mechanism of 1968 collective farms were given more power to manage their production and marketing. These changes allowed Hungary to achieve near self-sufficiency in food, but from the late 1970s low prices induced the peasants to reduce holdings of livestock, and shortages followed. In Czechoslovakia, financial problems led the regime to halt the movement towards collectivisation in the 1960s.

In East Germany land reform was an early item on the agenda: between 1945 and 1949 35 per cent of farmland was redistributed. In 1952 and 1953 Agricultural Production Cooperatives were established, modelled on Soviet collectives. These units became increasingly specialised and did enable the GDR to become self-sufficient in agriculture by the 1980s. The GDR's programme of collectivisation was extended between 1958 and 1960. Agricultural organisation was distinctive in that during the 1970s and 1980s a 'dual system' was fostered by which specialist crop-producing collectives were set up, including machine and tractor stations, whilst separate collectives specialised in livestock. However, farming suffered from a lack of investment, the farmers lacked motivation, and environmental damage was caused by soil erosion and neglect.

Large estates were confiscated in Romania and forced collectivisation began in 1948, to be completed by 1962. However, Romania resisted Soviet pressure to reduce its programme for industrialisation and concentrate on grain production, so as to become the granary for other Eastern Bloc states: the Romanian regime had no intention of becoming more dependent on powerful industrial neighbours. Bulgaria collectivised and did have one of the more agriculturally-orientated economies in the region. It also became in 1957 one of the first Eastern Bloc countries to extend welfare provision, including pensions, to collective farm workers. Nevertheless there was a crisis in 1962 when wheat had to be imported from Canada to make up for domestic shortfalls. Experiments in decentralising controls over agriculture were abandoned when events in Czechoslovakia in 1968 made such ventures dangerous. However, from 1973 there was a policy in Bulgaria of replacing traditional collective farms with large agro-industrial complexes, although, in contrast to Romania, the rights of peasants to farm small plots were guaranteed. The plots of land remained state-owned, but the private production they generated made a significant contribution to the economy: even in 1958 40 per cent of milk and 52 per cent of meat were produced privately, and the plots also accounted for one-third of all sheep and cattle.

Polish agriculture was least in step with the Soviet model. There was such resistance to the idea of collectivisation even among many Polish Communists that during Stalin's lifetime 75 per cent of farm land stayed in peasant hands. Stalin accepted the anomaly, declaring that 'Communism fits Poland like a saddle fits a cow.' The attitude seemed to be that as long as the Party stayed in control, it was better to accept certain 'deviations' than to insist on policies which would create mass resentment. Many of those farms that were collectivised in the early postwar years were disbanded in 1956. Privately-owned farms supplied 80 per cent of Poland's food, although state farms received four-fifths of total agricultural investment, and private farmers were forced to sell food to the state below production costs in order to have the right to buy fertiliser, seed, coal and cement. Food imports had to be increased by 400 per cent in the 1970s.

One feature common to rural life throughout the Eastern Bloc was a decline in the relative importance of the rural economy compared to industry, sometimes accompanied by a drift to the towns. 1.5 million Poles abandoned farming during Gierek's regime alone and there were similar shifts elsewhere: partly because farming was seen as unprofitable, partly because, whatever urban problems there might be, facilities and prospects of work in the towns seemed better. In Romania Ceauşescu's regime encouraged rural depopulation through its ruthless 'Systematisation Policy', introduced in 1974 but applied most rigorously in the 1980s: whole villages were destroyed at short notice in order to concentrate their populations in larger units. Peasants suffered rigid controls on their small private plots.

The percentage of the labour force employed in agriculture					
	1950	1960	1970	1978-80	1987-88
Czechoslovakia	38	26	19	13	12
GDR	24	18	13	11	11
Hungary	49	37	25	21	21
Poland	56	47	39	30	28
UK	6	2	2	1.6	

(Source: L.P. Morris, *Eastern Europe Since 1945*, London 1984.)

The percentage of the population classified as urban					
	1949-51	1960-64	1970	1980	1988
Czechoslovakia	51	48	62	73	76
GDR	71	73	74	76	77
Hungary	37	40	50	57	60
Poland	39	48	52	58	61

(Source: Morris.)

Collectivisation was not popular with many peasants, who felt little incentive to produce large surpluses. Whatever experiments were tried, the long-term record of agricultural production in Eastern and Central Europe was not impressive, and in this respect the region simply reflected what happened in the USSR itself.

3 Industry in the Eastern Bloc

KEY ISSUE What were the principal features of industrial organisation and practice in the Eastern Bloc economies?

The Eastern Bloc regimes initially adopted industrial policies based on the Soviet model. However, as with agriculture, there were divergencies as the economies matured and had to adapt to changing circumstances. Some economies, notably the East German and Czech ones, were progressing from a more developed base than others. The regimes were not necessarily free to implement policies as they chose: the USSR had views on what was good for its own economy and for the Eastern Bloc as a whole. Where a regime had conflicting views, as in the case of Romania, friction could result. In the long run none of the industrial policies adopted was completely successful in meeting the growing expectations of citizens. Ultimately they could not be persuaded by propaganda that the sacrifices involved in many of the economic policies adopted were in their interests.

Estimated annual growth rates in Gross National Product						
	1950-55	1955-60	1960-65	1965-70	1970-75	1975-80
Czechoslovakia	3.0	6.3	2.0	3.5	3.4	2.2
GDR	6.4	5.0	2.9	3.2	3.5	2.4
Hungary	4.7	4.6	4.3	3.1	3.4	2.3
Poland	4.6	4.5	4.1	3.8	6.6	0.9
	1980	1982	1984	1980-85	1986	1987
Czechoslovakia	1.7	1.4	2.2	1.4	2.1	1.3
GDR	2.4	0.0	3.0	1.7	1.5	2.2
Hungary	0.5	1.5	1.3	0.9	2.1	1.2
Poland	-3.2	-0.6	3.4	1.2	2.8	-2.5

(Source T.P. Alton, 'Comparison of overall economic performance in the East European countries' in (ed) R. Weichhardt, *The Economies of Eastern Europe Under Gorbachev's Influence*, Brussels 1989.)

a) Polish Industry

> **KEY ISSUE** How successful was the Polish economy under Communism?

This was particularly true in Poland. The Polish economy, devastated by war, could not afford the huge investment needed to make the First Five-Year Plan work. Between 1950 and 1953 inflation ran at 80 per cent. There was rationing and real wages fell. As the urban population expanded, so living and working conditions deteriorated. In 1956, in an attempt to increase motivation and productivity, some controls were relaxed; the number of targets was reduced; workers' bonuses were more closely allied to profits; and workers' councils were given more say in enterprise decisions. Bureaucratic conservatism and obstructionism defeated many of these reforms, as was often the case in Eastern Bloc states. 1960s Poland had one of the lowest growth rates in Europe. If the Government did not want to pass on to consumers the higher prices which peasants were demanding, food had to be subsidised. This was inefficient and costly. However, to cut subsidies provoked strikes and demonstrations. There would always be a dilemma for the Government unless there was the substantial economic growth which could pay for restructuring.

After 1970 Gierek adopted a more flexible approach in Poland: seeking closer economic ties with the West, allowing more initiative and modernising industry. However, important investment decisions were still made by the state, and the 1970s oil crisis frustrated plans for expansion. After a brief period of rising production and wages in the early 1970s, the pattern of growth was reversed and foreign debts mounted, to reach over six billion dollars by 1976. A massive rise in prices provoked strikes and demonstrations in 1976. In 1980 Gierek publicly acknowledged the failure of the Five-Year Plan. Managers were told to make individual wage settlements with their workers. Discontent led directly to the growth of the *Solidarity* movement. In the 1980s Jaruzelski's regime talked again of decentralisation and incentives. But rising prices, falling real wages and growing debts foreshadowed economic crisis. In the mid 1980s the Government encouraged Polish emigrés to return and establish private enterprises. Hundreds of these *Polonia* companies were set up, a tacit admission that Poland's socialist economy was not working. By 1987 the hard currency foreign debt stood at 40 billion dollars and inflation was running at 60 per cent a year. As elsewhere in the Eastern Bloc, mounting economic problems fuelled dissatisfaction with the ruling regime.

b) Czechoslovakian Industry

> **KEY ISSUE** What were the main features of Czechoslovakian industrial practice and how successful was the Czechoslovak economy?

The economic situation in Czechoslovakia was initially different from Poland. Living standards and levels of output were relatively high by Eastern Bloc levels, although Slovakia was the poorer part of the country. However, Czechoslovakia was subject to the rigours of Stalinist economics: by the end of 1948 80 per cent of industries and services were nationalised, and the remainder were taken over during the next four years. Plans for rapid growth took little account of the needs of consumers. Following Khrushchev's reforms in the USSR, the Czechoslovak regime made a half-hearted commitment to economic reform. The number of centrally-imposed targets was cut, and enterprises were given more say in investment decisions. But these changes were reversed in the 1960s, and growth rates suffered. The overambitious Third Five-Year Plan, set in 1960, was abandoned in 1962, as the growth in GNP declined to zero. Czechoslovakia became the first Eastern Bloc country to record an actual decline in National Income. The regime's promises of economic progress seemed hollow. As in other states, there was an influx of the rural population into the towns.

Recognising the need for decisive action, the Party employed the economist Otto Sik to draw up a reform programme. His 'New Economic Model' combined elements of central planning and a market economy. There was to be limited decentralisation of planning, enterprises would be given more freedom, and more realistic account would be taken of demand and production needs. Sik asserted that Marxist-Leninist theories had to be adapted. There was strong opposition from conservative bureaucrats and managers. Sik faced the problem of many reformers in the Eastern Bloc: resistance from an Establishment reluctant to change either out of ideological commitment or because it had a privileged stake in the existing system. Sik's conclusion was radical: economic reform would only succeed if combined with a measure of political reform - precisely what the Soviets would not allow in the following year. Sik declared:

1   The government decided that the city fathers had to do something to end the chaotic traffic jams in the streets of Prague. The Hall considered the matter for some time; finally someone proposed that we study the English system in order to find a sensible method of regulating traffic.
5   A commission was sent to London. It returned six months later. The first, rather surprising observation of the traffic experts was that in London they drive on the left. 'Ah,' the city fathers said, 'this may be the solution. So it was decreed that after a certain date everyone in Prague would have to drive on the left. The experts expressed doubt; if a funda-
10 mental change of this sort were carried out suddenly in a busy city like Prague, the result could be disastrous. So the city fathers formed a compromise solution. They decreed that the new   regulation would apply only to taxi-drivers. My plan has met a similar fate - they have strangled it by 'testing' it only in matters that are typical and of small
15 import. Whilst people have recognised the importance of changing the entire system, they do not want to do so everywhere.

In other words, reformers recognised the desirability of change, but were unwilling to gamble on radical measures which might upset the Establishment. Therefore partial reforms were adopted which did not work, and were often sabotaged by apathy or outright opposition.

When the Czechoslovak reformers of 1968 did progress from economic to political change, the USSR and its allies moved in to crush reform. After the USSR re-established its authority, the Stalinist model of centralised economic control, imposed targets and allocation of resources, was re-introduced in the early 1970s. This, plus lack of new investment, led to minimal growth rates, and the once prosperous Czechoslovakia slipped behind some of its neighbours. Soviet help, including subsidised oil deliveries, was necessary to stimulate modest growth. And yet Husák told the Central Committee in 1985 that despite Gorbachev's reforms in the USSR, 'We will not take the road of any of the market-oriented concepts that would weaken the system of socialist collective property and the party's leading role in the economy. We have had experience with this sort of thing.' When Husák finally felt obliged to make his own statement in favour of reform, in March 1987, it was too late to save his regime.

c) Hungary and the New Economic Mechanism

> **KEY ISSUE** What was distinctive about Hungary's New Economic Mechanism and how successful was it?

As in Czechoslovakia, the initial Hungarian experience of a Stalinist-type economy was not encouraging. Industry was nationalised, but falling wages led to strikes in 1953. The targets of the 1950-4 Plan were not met. Imre Nagy, in the wake of Soviet reforms after Stalin's death which put more emphasis on producing consumer goods, implemented a 'New Course'. Nagy conceded that 'we failed to realise the basic economic law of socialism - the constant raising of the standard of living of the population.'

Nagy's radical views contributed to his downfall. However, in the aftermath of 1956, his successor János Kádár also favoured economic reform as a means of trying to win legitimacy and popular support at a time of disillusionment following the crushing of the Hungarian Rising. The reforms were partly structural. Between 1958 and 1962 many enterprises were merged in an attempt to achieve greater efficiency. In 1965 the Central Committee approved a draft plan for modernisation, and the result was the New Economic Mechanism (NEM), which came into force in January 1968. It was an ambitious attempt to create a 'socialist market economy', combining a self-regulating market economy with an authoritarian political regime. Two of the cornerstones of Stalinist economics - central planning and the central allocation of resources - were abandoned. Targets based on quantity alone were abolished. More experts were to be involved in decision-making. Enterprises were now expected to make profits, although they were protected from fluctuations in world prices. Small private enterprises were legalised and encouraged. Long-term planning and the central allocation of investment funds now had a much smaller place. Some prices were fixed, some were entirely determined by the market, and some were allowed to fluctuate between limits determined by the state.

The aim was to eliminate central control over the manufacture of capital goods but not consumer goods: capital goods were sold through wholesale enterprises at a price agreed by the buyer and seller, whilst consumer goods and services were still regulated by the Government. The reforms did not amount to the introduction of a western-style market economy, but were nevertheless a considerable departure from the Stalinist economic model in place elsewhere in the Eastern Bloc. The reforms aroused opposition, but also influenced a later generation of Soviet reformers like Andropov and Gorbachev and were the most radical reforms attempted in the Eastern Bloc before the fall of Communism. Ironically, the NEM was begun in the same year that the USSR crushed the Czechoslovak reform movement. The message seemed to be that economic reform might be attempted, but not significant political changes.

NEM was initially successful. The first ten years saw growth rates of almost 7 per cent a year, a high figure by international standards. Real wages doubled. But ultimately NEM failed to sustain growth levels, which by the late 1970s had fallen to less than 3 per cent a year. The Government was forced to implement a tough austerity programme to reduce domestic consumption. In 1982 it joined the International Monetary Fund and the World Bank in order to acquire international assistance.

Problems led to further restructuring. In the Kádár era there was a policy battle in the Central Committee between the centralisers and those who maintained that NEM would only flourish if there were further moves towards a market economy. For a time it seemed that the recentralisers would be successful: in 1973 some 'privileged' enterprises, accounting for over half of national production, were established and freed from the requirement to respond to market forces. A new State Planning Committee was given increased powers. However, in 1975 some hardliners were removed from the Central Committee and in 1979 the basic principles of NEM were reaffirmed. Living standards were only raised by means of massive Soviet aid and reductions in military spending.

The private sector in Hungary expanded at the expense of the state sector, despite ever increasing subsidies to the latter. By 1985 there were 600 small cooperatives and 30,000 work partnerships. Two thirds of these were Enterprise Economic Work Partnerships, a form of organisation which permitted groups of workers to use their workplaces outside normal hours to do extra work on a profit-making individual basis. Since 'moonlighting' was common in all Eastern Bloc economies, this was simply an official sanctioning of what happened anyway, and most workers put more effort into their after-hours work.

Substantial and effective reform of the Hungarian economy was hampered by entrenched corruption and bureaucratic obstructionism. However, there were some important developments in the 1980s. In 1982-83 enterprises were given permission to issue bonds, and in 1985 they were given virtual autonomy. Enterprises were allowed to choose between being managed by an enterprise council or an elected leadership. Joint-stock companies were permitted in 1986, competing banks were introduced in 1987, and share-holding by individuals was legalised in 1989. But large-state monopoly enterprises became ever more powerful, whilst hard currency debts escalated and inflation rose. By the end of the 1980s NEM had proved a failure and Hungary was left with an increasingly obsolete industrial structure. This failure was ultimately responsible for the downfall of Communism in Hungary.

d) The East German 'Economic Miracle'

> **KEY ISSUE**   To what extent did East Germany experience an 'economic miracle'?

Like Hungary, East Germany adapted the Stalinist economic model without destroying the basic principle of state control. The East German economy was distinctive in the Eastern Bloc in several important respects. It was one of the more developed economies in the region before the Communist takeover. Secondly, it was treated as a source of reparations for damage inflicted on the USSR during the War. The USSR helped itself to factories, railway stock and machinery well into the 1950s. Another distinctive feature of the economy was the fact that until the mid 1950s only property identified as belonging to Nazis had been nationalised. Many factories retained a semi-private status: although the state provided capital and received some of the profits, the owner of the enterprise remained the managing director. In the early 1970s 15 per cent of the industrial workforce still worked in such enterprises.

The German leader Walter Ulbricht was a political hardliner but was ready to promote economic and technological reform in order to make the GDR an advanced industrial society. It was not an easy task. Within two years of joining COMECON in 1950, 75 per cent of the GDR's trade was with fellow Eastern Bloc members, and only one tenth with West Germany. The GDR struggled to make up its disadvantages compared with the West. It was only half the size of West Germany, and one fifth of the size of prewar Germany. It had few natural resources apart from brown coal and had lost the valuable coalfields of Upper Silesia. The entire GDR accounted for only one quarter of prewar Germany's industrial and agricultural output. Despite this, the GDR did become a major economic power.

In keeping with Stalinist practice, planning was ambitious, with an emphasis upon heavy industry as well as providing for reparations to the USSR. The first Five-Year Plan of January 1951 aimed to increase industrial production by 90 per cent and labour productivity by 70 per cent. However, the 1953 riots resulting from popular discontent with living conditions prompted the regime to introduce the 'New Course'. This reduced the targets for heavy industry, put more emphasis on consumer goods, and subsidised prices. The USSR began to give credit to the GDR and ceased extracting reparations.

The Second Five-Year Plan of 1956 set the ambitious target of overtaking West Germany economically by 1961. However, an average growth rate of 4 per cent a year was well below West German levels. Economic progress was hampered by low levels of investment and over-rigid economic management. Consequently the leadership continued to experiment with variants of economic planning. The 'New System of Economic Planning and Management' (NES) was implemented in 1964, with features distinctive in the Eastern Bloc. Enterprises were given more decision-making powers and financial incentives and credit opportunities were given to profitable firms. Associations called VVBs were set up: these 'socialist corporations' planned, coordinated and controlled production of all enterprises in a particular branch of the economy. The chemical, energy and electrical engineering sectors were affected first. The VVBs controlled research and development and were expected to include variables such as profit and costs in their calculations. There was a formula to determine how profits should be distributed once taxation had been accounted for.

Targets were still set centrally and there was central allocation of resources. The state plan had to be fulfilled. Nevertheless, it was a radical step to make profit a prominent factor in economic performance. Quality was considered as important as quantity and the fulfilment of quotas. Some of the more radical features of the system were soon altered. In 1967 NES was renamed the 'Economic System of Socialism', and certain sectors of the economy were given priority over others, showing an renewed emphasis upon planning and recentralisation. In these respects the GDR's economy still retained strong similarities with the economies of the USSR and other Eastern Bloc countries.

Economic progress presented a mixed picture. Economic growth was substantial in the mid 1960s, but whilst the more favoured economic sectors prospered, others suffered from shortages of supplies, particularly raw materials from other COMECON countries. By the 1980s industry made up over 75 per cent of the GDR's GNP, and employed over half the work force. Almost two million workers were in mechanical engineering, electronics and chemicals, which together accounted for half of industrial production. Nevertheless, industry was technologically backward in comparison with Western European economies, for example in the car industry. Economic problems increased from the mid 1970s, although the regime's propaganda hid many of the effects from its own population and the outside world. Under Honecker, economic policy was ultimately unsuccessful. He was obsessed with autarchy, or economic self-sufficiency, and emphasised state planning. The plans for the 1970s set more modest targets, and tried to encourage more women into full-time work, but the economy suffered from the world economic crisis of 1973-4, particularly since the GDR was dependent on imports of fuel and raw materials. By the late 1970s imports were double exports, and the national debt - over 20 billion dollars by 1981 - was second only to Poland's among COMECON countries.

The regime's measures to maintain economic growth failed in the long term. During the 1970s 130 *kombinatts* were set up. These were enterprises responsible to state ministries and charged with fulfilling the Plan, but they were also expected to find more efficient approaches. However, inaccurate planning, wasteful use of raw materials, high energy consumption and a failure to invest in the latest technology - failings of all the Eastern Bloc economies - resulted in a falling behind the West in terms of labour productivity and living standards. This despite the fact that the GDR benefitted from a special trade relationship with West Germany and access to European Union markets, in which it did not have to suffer quotas or tariffs. The GDR earned huge sums from charges for transit across its territory to West Berlin, and also received payment for the release of political prisoners. Yet large credits had to be obtained from West Germany in the early 1980s to avert a major crisis. Compared to some Communist economies, the GDR had a good economic record, but the standard of living of East German citizens was only half that of their Western counterparts. Prospects were further damaged by a fall in the GDR's population from 18.5 million in 1946 to 17 million by 1965, due both to the emigration of young people and a low rate of natural increase. Half the workforce was female, and the state had to provide extensive childcare facilities and attempt to improve housing. This policy had some success, but further encouraged migration to towns from neglected rural areas.

The East German population was conscious of the better quality of life in the West, since it had access to West German television with its emphasis on consumerism, and there were increasing numbers of visitors from the West. Growth in the domestic economy fell to 2.1 per cent by 1989, well short of the target. The focus of economic activity shifted ever westwards: about 20 per cent of the GDR's trade was with West Germany, one third with the European Union, and only 22 per cent with the USSR. This contributed to the regime's desire for better relations with the West. However, whereas the relative prosperity of the GDR had enabled the regime to maintain its legitimacy, that prosperity was disappearing quickly, with disastrous effects for the regime.

e) Industry in Romania and Bulgaria

> **KEY ISSUE** What were the principal features of industrial organisation in Romania and Bulgaria and how much industrial progress was there?

Romania and Bulgaria possessed less developed economies than their partners in the Eastern Bloc, and followed the more orthodox model of a Stalinist industrial economy. Ironically, Romania pursued its programme of industrialisation in the face of Soviet disapproval, since Moscow wanted the Romanians to concentrate on producing food for their socialist neighbours. Romania was therefore forced to cultivate foreign contacts to secure loans. However, a planned export drive did not take off, and in 1976 Romania, an oil-producing country, had to start importing oil. The 'New Economic and Financial Mechanism' of 1978 expected enterprises to be self-reliant and cost-efficient, but at the same time they were expected to conform and were subject to centralised control. As growth rates declined in the late 1970s, imports were curbed so as to reduce hard currency debts. Austerity measures unprecedented in the Eastern Bloc were introduced in 1982 and 1983. Petrol, meat, bread, flour, sugar, milk and domestic fuel supplies were all rationed. By the time of Ceauşescu's overthrow in 1989 the Romanian economy was on a downward spiral.

The Bulgarian economy was also organised on the Stalinist model. After the moderate Third Five-Year Plan of 1958-62 the regime increased the targets considerably. There were few signs of strain until the 1970s, but then there was a marked slowdown in growth. Because Bulgaria did not have a strong industrial base, coal, iron and oil were imported from the USSR. In an attempt to become more self-sufficient, the huge Kremikovsti steel and iron complex was built in 1962 and 1963 near Sofia, with Soviet aid. However, almost half the population was still engaged in farming and industry, although it was still necessary to import foreign wheat when there were domestic short-falls. An unguarded Bulgarian citizen was heard to observe: 'No nation is working so hard and so strenuously as ours, yet none lives so miserably.'

In the 1980s Bulgaria adopted its own 'New Economic Mechanism'. Small semi-autonomous units were encouraged within larger ones and banking facilities were extended. However, the degree of reform and experimentation was limited even in comparison with the more developed Eastern Bloc economies, and this was an important factor in the eventual demise of Bulgarian Communism, as it was to be a major contributory factor to the crisis facing all the Eastern Bloc regimes in this period.

Making notes on 'Economic Systems'

This chapter focuses on the economic systems and economic history of the various Eastern Bloc states. Your notes should concentrate on picking out the main features of the Stalinist economic system; how they were adapted over time in each country; and ultimately the degree to which the regimes' economic policies were or were not successful. Take note of both agricultural and industrial policies, their impact on ordinary people, and where possible compare the experiences of the different countries.

Summary Diagram

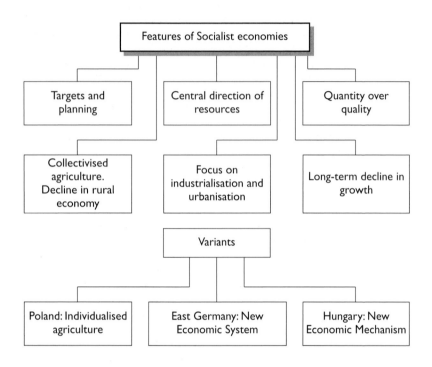

Answering structured questions and essay questions on 'Economic Systems'

Essays on economic affairs may be about the Eastern Bloc generally, or less commonly, about a particular country. The following are examples of each:

1. **a)** Outline the main developments in the economies of any **TWO** of the following countries between the establishment of Communist control and the 1980s: Poland; Czechoslovakia; Hungary; East Germany;

   b) Examine the similarities and differences between the two economies you have selected during this period.

2. The 'East German economic miracle.' To what extent was the GDR's economy really so successful between the establishment of the Communist regime and its overthrow in the 1980s?

In part (a) of essay 1 you are required to outline economic developments in two countries. You should give the main developments briefly throughout the whole period, and ensure that you include both agriculture and industry, although not necessarily to the same extent.

It would also be valid here to refer briefly to COMECON. The key phrase in part (b) is 'Examine the similarities and differences.' Some are obvious: for example the fact that much of Poland's agriculture remained uncollectivised. Ensure that you do consider both differences and similarities, and remember that economic policies did sometimes alter over several years, even though the fundamentals of the Stalinist command economy remained in place. For example, at different periods in their histories both Hungary and the GDR attempted changes in their industrial organisation which were quite radical by orthodox Communist standards. The question is so worded that you may focus both on structures and the degree of success or failure - the important thing is to plan your approach before you begin, in order to make your answer manageable.

The key phrases in essay 2 are the quotation 'East German economic miracle' and 'really so successful.' You will need to outline the principal economic developments in more detail than, for example, in essay 1; and then discuss how successful they actually were. 'Success' is not always an easy concept to apply. The economy ran into serious problems, some of the regime's own making, some beyond its control. Given the difficulties experienced in the early years, for example the loss of industrial territory and the massive reparations extracted by the USSR, the GDR's economic recovery was remarkable. In some respects it was the success story of the Eastern Bloc. However, the achievements did not all last, and an economic decline set in - hence the concept of 'miracle' might be questioned. Since 'success' is a relative term, there is no definitive answer, but be prepared to back up your arguments with evidence. You might make the point that had the regime's economic achievements been so miraculous, it is unlikely that the regime would have collapsed so easily in 1989, but for this question do not become too heavily involved in political issues unless you can clearly relate them to your analysis.

Source-based questions on 'Economic Systems'

1. Reform in Czechoslovakia.

Read the extract by Otto Sik on the limitations of reform on page 67. Answer the following questions:

a) Using your own knowledge, explain why economic and political reforms were increasingly seen as necessary in 1960s Czechoslovakia. (5 marks)

b) Summarise the message that Sik was trying to put across in this extract. (4 marks)

c) Using the extract and your own knowledge, explain why Sik's reform proposals were not accepted. (6 marks)

d) How valuable is this extract to historians as evidence of the underlying reasons for the events in Czechoslovakia in 1968? (5 marks)

6 Revolt

POINTS TO CONSIDER

This chapter will introduce you to the major challenges to Communist rule in the Eastern Bloc between the establishment of Communist control and its overthrow in the late 1980s. Your aim on first reading the chapter should be to understand the causes of the challenges to Communist rule in Hungary, Czechoslovakia and Poland between 1956 and the early 1980s, how the challenges were dealt with, and the significance of the challenges for the countries concerned and for the region as a whole.

KEY DATES

1953 Serious disturbances in East Germany
1956 Hungarian Rising
1968 Dubček became Czechoslovak Party leader
Prague Spring and invasion of Czechoslovakia
1980 Founding of *Solidarity*
Martial law declared in Poland

1 Conformity and Conflict

> **KEY ISSUE** How did the regimes of the Eastern Bloc try to ensure political conformity, and why did challenges to the regimes nevertheless occur?

As explained in earlier chapters, the structure of the Communist-controlled states established throughout the Eastern Bloc from the late 1940s onwards was such as to provide a strong disincentive to overt opposition. Manipulated elections in which only approved candidates were allowed to stand made free expression of public opinion impossible and free debate in parliaments unlikely. The use of propaganda and the apparatus of police states combined to discourage peaceful opposition to the regimes. There was often political infighting among Communists, and, as we have seen, these sometimes led to purges which could result in demotions, imprisonment or even death for the losers. Ordinary people intent on getting on with their lives developed an apathy towards political activity. Provided that they showed at least an outward conformity citizens were left in peace, certainly after the excesses of the Stalinist period. Massive shows of public approval of the various regimes was only occasionally called for, to celebrate some special event or achievement or to demonstrate electoral support.

The threat of direct intervention, led or organised by the USSR, was present in the background for those regimes which threatened the unity of the Eastern Bloc or appeared in danger of losing their hold on the general population. Yet there were a few occasions when discontent or a desire for change were serious enough to cause major confrontations challenging the status quo in Eastern and Central Europe. Sometimes these occasions originated from developments within Communist parties, sometimes from outside, and sometimes a combination of both. Until the collapse of all the Communist regimes in the late 1980s, none of the revolts against 'traditional' Communist rule succeeded in destroying the system, but the experience did have major repercussions and remained as a warning to the regimes that they could not take the status quo for granted.

There were danger signs quite early on. In May 1953 the GDR's leader Ulbricht ordered an increase in production, despite the still relatively fragile state of his country's economy. The USSR tried to persuade him to amend his policy, but on the day that the new decrees were to take effect, 16 June 1953, strikes and demonstrations broke out in industrial centres. Ulbricht misjudged the seriousness of the threat. East Berlin had to be declared in a state of siege, and the disturbances spread throughout the country. Soviet troops were needed to restore order. 25,000 people were arrested and over 400 executed. Thereafter the East German regime employed a huge network of police and informers to keep control of the situation, and relied upon improving living conditions to produce a docile population. The policy worked in that after 1953 the East German population was relatively obedient. Although there was evidence of increasing dissatisfaction with the regime from the 1970s, it was not necessarily aimed at the very existence of the East German state. The 1953 riots were prompted by economic unrest. By the 1970s, it was remarkable that the existence of the GDR had come to be taken for granted in so many quarters. Opposition was usually aimed at reforming the regime rather than overthrowing it.

2 The Hungarian Rising

> **KEY ISSUE** What were the causes of the 1956 Hungarian Rising, why did it fail, and what was its significance?

a) The Background to Revolt

In the summer of 1956 there were workers' riots in Poznan, Poland. But of more significance for the Eastern Bloc as a whole were events in Hungary that autumn. When Imre Nagy was expelled from the Party in 1955 (see page 45) he continued to hope for rehabilitation, but argued in a dangerously radical way. In a document, *On Communism*,

Nagy declared that following the Soviet model of Socialism had simply led other regimes down the path of authoritarianism backed up by force. Nations should develop their own paths to Socialism 'by systematically decreasing the use of force [and] utilising democratic forms and methods in the interest of close cooperation on the widest possible scale with the masses of working people'. From the Soviet standpoint, just as dangerous was Nagy's desire for Hungary to be a neutral power, like neighbouring Austria. That would strike a blow at the foundations of the recently formed Warsaw Pact and the Eastern Bloc's defence structure.

Nagy claimed that his views were not unmarxist. However, since Hungarian dissidents looked to him for inspiration, he was bound to be suspect to the regime. The most significant dissident group was the Petofi Circle, which had developed by 1956 into a large pressure group making demands for Nagy's restoration to power. Meetings and strikes increased throughout Hungary. Rákosi's response was to implement more repression and arrange a Central Committee Plenum to call for the arrest of active dissidents. But the Soviet leadership doubted Rákosi's ability to keep control and distrusted his proposals for a new crackdown. One of the Soviet leaders Mikoyan attended the Plenum and Rákosi was dismissed. He was replaced by Ernő Gerő, regarded as a Soviet ally. He proposed to reactivate the Patriotic People's Front and implement some economic reforms. After discussions with Moscow, Nagy was invited back into the Party on 13 October 1956.

Khrushchev's hopes that events in Hungary would stabilise were dashed. Popular protests became more pronounced. The Petofi Circle called for a mass demonstration on 23 October to demand the withdrawal of Soviet troops from Hungary and Nagy's appointment as Government leader. Nagy himself was hesitant to commit himself to either side. The demonstration went ahead despite a Government ban, and this act of defiance was the real beginning of the Hungarian Rising. The Communist leadership was unsure of how to respond. Nagy agreed to appeal for calm, but was in a difficult position: he wanted the support of both the people and the Party, but the popular mood was against the Party.

b) The Rising

On the same day as Nagy's appeal, Gerő denounced the demonstrators in a radio speech. This further inflamed the situation: demonstrators flocked to the radio station and captured it on the following day after violent clashes. At the same time Soviet tanks, requested by Gerő, entered Budapest. Nagy had no part in this decision. It was the start of four days of bitter fighting. Although Nagy had already been asked to form a government, he was still waiting to be co-opted into the Politburo, a necessary precondition to becoming Prime Minister.

Emotions were running high, as evident in the tone and radical nature of the demands in this resolution broadcast by a workers' council on 25 October, during the fighting:

1 End the massacre of Hungarians in Budapest! Do not believe deceptions! Let them withdraw Soviet troops from Hungary! Strike ... We have had enough - enough of the autocracy of certain leaders. We too want socialism but according to our own special Hungarian conditions,
5 which reflect the interests of the Hungarian working class and the Hungarian nation, and our most sacred national sentiments.

We demand that all persons who compromised themselves by the cult of personality be eliminated immediately ...

We demand that those Communists and non-Communists be given
10 the most important positions in government and party life who, in following the principles of proletarian internationalism, honour above all else our Hungarian national traditions and our thousand-year history.

We demand the revision of the institutions of the state security authority and the elimination immediately of all leaders and func-
15 tionaries who are compromised ... We demand an increase of real wages.

We believe our demands will be realised when our parliament ceases to be an electoral machine, and the members of parliament cease being yes-men.

On 25 October Moscow agreed that János Kádár should replace Gerö as Party Secretary, with Nagy as Prime Minister. The next day Nagy appealed to the Patriotic People's Front to recommend the make-up of a new Government. He then appealed for a ceasefire and the withdrawal of Soviet troops. Nagy strongly praised the Hungarian fighters and in a radio broadcast of 28 October declared:

1 The Government condemns the viewpoints according to which the present formidable movement is counterrevolution ... Reactionary and counterrevolutionary elements had penetrated into the movement with the aim of overthrowing the popular democratic regime.
5 But it is also indisputable that in these stirrings a great national and democratic movement, embracing and unifying all our people, developed with elemental force. This movement aims at guaranteeing our national freedom, independence and sovereignty, of advancing our society, our economic and political system on the way of democracy - for this is the
10 only foundation for socialism in our country ...

The situation was further aggravated by the fact that up to the very last, the party leadership had not decided to break finally with the old and criminal policy. It is this above all which led to the tragic fratricidal fight in which so many patriots died on both sides. In the course of these
15 battles was born the government of democratic national unity, independence, and socialism which will become the true expression of the will of the people ...

    The Government wishes to rest in the first place on the support of
the fighting Hungarian working class, but also, of course, on the support
20 of the entire Hungarian working population.

Nagy went on to form a multi-party Government on 30 October, a
move opposed by both Kádár and Moscow. Hungarian rebels set up a
Revolutionary Committee of Defence which urged that Hungary
should leave the Warsaw Pact and proclaim neutral status. Nagy did
not veto this declaration. This was the final straw for the Soviets. They
invaded Hungary on 4 November. Khrushchev had already secured
support for his actions from other Eastern Bloc leaders afraid for their
own positions should a wave of disaffection spread across their own
borders from Hungary. The Soviets claimed that counter-revolution
was about to break out in Hungary, although Nagy strongly denied
the existence of such a threat.

    Despite active resistance to the Soviet invasion by many
Hungarians, the outcome was not in doubt. Hungary got no support
from the outside world. The West was embroiled in the Suez crisis
caused by the intervention of Britain and France against Nasser's
Egypt; and, in any case, Western powers were not prepared to actively
intervene in what most serious commentators accepted was a Soviet
sphere of influence. Whilst Kádár formed a new Government with
Soviet backing, and he formed a new Hungarian Socialist Workers'

The remains of Stalin's statue in Budapest, October 1956

Party (HSWP), Nagy took refuge in the Yugoslav embassy. He was then abandoned by Tito. Having been promised safe conduct by Kádár, Nagy was captured by Soviet troops and executed after the Rising was suppressed. Kádár told the world in a speech:

1 By his [Nagy's] impotence and passivity he actually camouflaged and protected the murderous counter-revolutionary white terror ... If he was powerless he should have resigned and told the country and the world that counter-revolutionaries were massacring the Communists
5 and other progressive patriots, workers and intellectuals in the streets of Budapest.

3,000 people were killed during the Rising and 13,000 wounded. 2,000 were later executed. 200,000 Hungarians fled to the West during the Rising and its immediate aftermath. Their presence abroad ensured that emotions continued to run high.

The Hungarian Rising was significant not just for Hungary, where it ushered in the long period of authoritarian rule by Kádár, but for the rest of the Eastern Bloc. It showed how far the Soviets were prepared to go to enforce their vision of the region. It served as a warning for years to come of the likely consequences if regimes deviated too far from the orthodox Kremlin position, particularly if they dabbled in political reform or permitted opposition to develop. The Rising was

Hungarian refugees cross the frontier into exile, 1956

by far the most serious clash between what was seen by Hungarians and the West on one hand as brutal Soviet repression and the crushing of the aspirations of ordinary Hungarians; and, on the other hand, was seen by the Kremlin as counter-revolution or the beginnings of a major crack in the Warsaw Pact. The USSR was not prepared to see its defence strategy upset or encouragement be given to opponents of one-party Communist rule elsewhere. Existing Cold War tensions simply added to outside interest in the events. The Soviets regarded Western indignation as hypocritical propaganda, and in any case regarded Hungary as their sphere of influence.

'Normality' was imposed on Hungary by the Kádár regime:

1 On 6 January 1957, after several postponements, the Kádár Government issued its long-awaited declaration of policy. It comes as a bucket of cold water upon the Hungarian nation. The revolution is labelled as a Fascist uprising and Imre Nagy is called a traitor ... 'the
5 stationing of Russian troops in Hungary is necessary to protect the country from possible imperialist attacks from abroad' ... Hungarian foreign policy would be based 'on the alliance with the Soviet Union and other Communist countries' ... No old parties would be allowed to re-form ... Events had come full circle. The clock has been put back,
10 Hungary is where she was before the revolution - indeed, a few steps farther back. As far as the Russians are concerned the revolution never happened.
(G. Mikes, *The Hungarian Revolution*, Andre Deutsch 1957.)

3 The 'Prague Spring' in Czechoslovakia

> **KEY ISSUE** What led to the 1968 crisis in Czechoslovakia and why did attempts at reform fail?

a) Novotný and Dubček

There were obvious parallels between Hungary in 1956 and Czechoslovakia in 1968, although events in the latter were far less bloody. In 1948, following the resignation of Beneš, Gottwald became President. After Gottwald's death in 1953, Antonín Zápotocký became Party leader, followed by Antonín Novotný in 1957. Novotný was a hardliner, whose reputation for conservatism, inflexibility and unscrupulousness led to increasing complaints from Slovakian Communists against Czech domination of the state and Party machines. Novotný's 1960 Constitution abolished most Slovak institutions on the premise that 'changes in Slovak national organs will be based on the fact that central direction of the whole life of our society according to a single nationwide plan is progressively deepening' - Communist jargon for the pretence that Communist states had done away with internal nationalist rivalries. At the time the policy was not challenged by promi-

---

BIOGRAPHY: ANTONÍN NOVOTNÝ

Novotný was born into a Prague working-class family. He became a founder member of the Czech Communist Party at the age of 17. He fought in the resistance during the Second World War, was captured by the Germans, and spent 1941-45 in Mauthausen concentration camp. He became First Secretary of the Party and President in 1957, holding both posts until he was ousted by reformers in 1968. In February he unsuccessfully tried to persuade the army to occupy Prague in an attempt to halt the reforms. Novotný was suspended from the Party in 1968, rehabilitated in 1971, but not given office again before his death in 1975.

---

nent Slovakian politicians, but it was to cause considerable resentment against Novotný. Novotný was also ordered by an exasperated Khrushchev to correct the 'errors of the fifties': a reference to the fact that Novotný resisted attempts by destalinisers to rehabilitate victims of the purges and to initiate economic reform, and indeed initiated new purges. However, he failed to remove his main critics.

It was rumoured that the Soviets were considering Novotný's removal. However, Brezhnev was busy consolidating his own position within the USSR. When Brezhnev visited Czechoslovakia in December 1967, he responded to Novotný's appeal for help against internal threats with the blunt retort: 'It's your affair.' Novotný succumbed to pressure from his own Party to resign the leadership in January 1968. Brezhnev may have regretted his response, since he soon faced a challenge in Czechoslovakia to Soviet authority itself.

Novotný's successor was Alexander Dubček, First Secretary of the Slovak Communist Party since 1963. Novotný had opposed his promotion then on the grounds that Dubček was a 'Slovak Nationalist', despite the fact that Dubček had consistently spoken against independent rights for Slovaks. Dubček had written in a news-paper article in 1954:

> 1 The organising element of this epoch in the life of our nation is the Czechoslovak Communist Party and its faithful collaborator the Slovak Party ... By broadening the merciless fight against bourgeois-nationalism and standardbearers, who were discovered and condemned as enemies
> 5 of the Party and the people, our Party played its part in strengthening and educating our people. It educated Slovaks in this spirit of Czechoslovak nationalism.

Dubček's language was that of a loyal and orthodox Communist, not that of a liberal reformer as he was later portrayed in some Western quarters. There were rumours that Dubček had made an agreement with Brezhnev in 1967 guaranteeing a peaceful settlement of any future difficulties between the two countries. Dubček considered himself a loyal ally of the USSR. Where he differed from Novotný was that he was used to compromise, having had practice at trying to appease the Slovaks, who were impatient at the slow progress of reform and their lack of recognition. Novotný, in contrast, had repeatedly refused them concessions. Novotný's enforced resignation increased the pressure for more change, including from Dubček's more radical supporters. In March 1968 an emergency meeting of the Warsaw Pact in Dresden warned about 'anti-socialist' elements in Czechoslovakia. Gomulka and Ulbricht in particular were concerned about the spread of reformist ideas to their own countries. Brezhnev urged Dubček to quieten calls for reform in the Czechoslovak press, but the press only criticised Dubček for timidity.

Reform went ahead. Victims of earlier purges were rehabilitated and censorship was abolished in June 1968. Novotný relinquished the presidency to Luvík Svoboda, a retired general who had assisted the Communist takeover years before and was trusted by the Soviets. In April 1968 the Party published its 'Action Programme'. The aim was to build a 'new profoundly democratic model of Czechoslovak socialism, conforming to Czechoslovak conditions.' There was a conscious harking back to Imre Nagy's ideas of the early 1950s: Dubček absorbed Nagy's notion of the 'democratic' party, one in which individual members and organisations would all have equal status. The Party did not have an automatic right to a monopoly of power: 'The party's goal is not to become a universal "caretaker" of society ... its mission lies primarily in arousing socialist initiative ... in winning over

BIOGRAPHY: ALEXANDER DUBČEK

Dubček's father was a minor official, and the family lived in the USSR between 1925 and 1938 because he wanted to help in the Soviet industrialisation drive. The young Dubček lived through Stalin's terror without apparently having any doubts about the Stalinist system. Back home, he was an early recruit to the Slovak Communist Party, formed in 1939. He worked for a time in a Skoda arms factory. During the War he fought against the German occupiers in the 1944 Slovak Rising.

After the War Dubček progressed through the Party ranks, avoiding the purges of 1948-54, and attending the Higher Party School in Moscow between 1953 and 1958. He became First Secretary of the Slovak Communist Party in 1963, and of the Czechoslovakian Party in January 1968.

Following the Soviet invasion, Dubček resigned as First Secretary in April 1969. He was sent as ambassador to Turkey, and was expelled from the Party in 1970. Dubček worked in relative obscurity as an inspector for forestry in Bratislava, periodically harassed by Husák's regime. He emerged into the limelight again after the fall of the Communists, to be elected as speaker of the federal assembly in 1989.

all workers by persuasion and example.' The Programme continued:

1   The main thing is to reform the whole political system so that it will
    permit the dynamic development of socialist social relations, combine
    broad democracy with a scientific, highly qualified management,
    strengthen the social order, stabilise socialist relations and maintain
5   social discipline. The basic structure of the political system must, at the
    same time, provide firm guarantees against a return to the old methods
    of subjectivism and highhandedness from a position of power ... polit-
    ical parties in our country cannot exclude common-interest organisa-
    tions of workers and other working people from directly influencing
10 state policy, its creation and application ... Legal norms must guarantee
    more exactly the freedom of speech of minority interests and opinions
    also ... The Party policy is based on the principle that no undue concen-
    tration of power must occur, throughout the state machinery, in one
    sector, one body, or in a single individual ...
15 The development of international economic relations will continue
    to be based on economic cooperation with the Soviet Union and the
    other socialist countries.

It was the radical nature of this Programme, and Soviet fears that it
might be accepted by the forthcoming Czechoslovakian Party
Congress, that eventually prompted the USSR to invade.

Dubček was optimistic in believing that the Communist Party could
maintain its leading role in society whilst encouraging genuine
popular participation of different groups. He was not renowned for
having original political ideas and was perhaps aware of his own limitations, which is why he later encouraged a perception of himself as a
surprise and reluctant compromise candidate for the leadership.
Dubček encouraged intellectuals and journalists to make constructive
criticism, at the same time as he emphasised his own support for all
things Soviet - surely a contradictory position since by 1968 he was,
for example, arguing for the separation of Party and State, which was
certainly not Soviet policy.

Dubček explicitly linked political sterility with economic shortcom-
ings. He claimed that bureaucracy had destroyed 'socialist democracy'. Reformers took over key posts, although the intention was still
to reform the Party from within, not take away all its power.

Dubček encountered the problems of most reformers in authoritarian societies: having stimulated popular hopes for change, he could
not control the rising flood of popular expectations without resorting
to the methods of the police state which he now disowned. In June
1968 60 intellectuals signed the '2,000 Words' document which urged
resistance to any attempts by the authorities to stop reform, and called
for strikes and boycotts to force the government into a rigorous purge
of Novotnýites in the Party, who thus far had been largely untouched
by the 'Prague Spring'. There was a widespread feeling that
Czechoslovakians could overturn 20 years of repression:

I   'Historical events usually imitate one another without much talent, but
    in Czechoslovakia, as I see it, history staged an unprecedented experi-
    ment. Instead of the standard pattern of one group of people (a class, a
    nation) rising up against another, all the people (an entire generation)
  5 revolted against their own youth. Their goal was to recapture and tame
    the deed they had created, and they almost succeeded.'
    (Milan Kundera, *The Book of Laughter and Forgetting*, Random House
    1980)

Warsaw Pact leaders issued further warnings to the Czechoslovak
leadership in May and June 1968. A letter was sent in July insisting
that the Czechoslovak Government reassert its authority over the
media and organisations.

b) Invasion and 'Normalisation'

The Soviet and Czechoslovak leaders met in Slovakia between 29 July
and 1 August 1968. The Czechoslovak leaders repeated pledges of
loyalty and agreed to suppress independent political organisations.
This did not satisfy the Pact's leaders, and on the night of 20-21 August
200,000 troops from the USSR, East Germany, Hungary, Poland and
Bulgaria invaded Czechoslovakia. The Kremlin declared that Socialism
in Czechoslovakia was under threat, since Dubček had lost control of
the Party, which had lost control of the nation. Dubček was portrayed
as a weak leader who had allowed counterrevolutionary influences to
undermine his authority. The reality was that Dubček had limited
support within his own Party, had no coherent programme, and gave
the impression that he was carried along by events.

The USSR hoped to set up a collaborationist Czechoslovakian
Government, but not enough conservatives came forward and the
Soviets were aware of popular support for Dubček. They decided
instead on negotiation with the existing leadership. President Svoboda
negotiated in Moscow between 23 and 26 August. Other leaders were
arrested and taken first to Poland and then to the Ukraine. The
Czechoslovak leadership was divided: Svoboda and Husák supported
concessions. Dubček wavered but eventually gave in, probably afraid of
bloodshed in Czechoslovakia if the leadership held out. The Moscow
Agreements were drawn up, and were to be broadcast by Dubček on his
return home. A Soviet delegation arrived in Prague to implement
changes. The terms essentially meant 'Normalisation': a reversal of
recent political reforms, ensuring the monopoly of power by the
Communist Party; a purge of reformers; and the appointment to the
Government of those 'who stood firm on the position of Marxism-
Leninism.' There was to be closer Soviet supervision of Czechoslovakia.

Dubček remained as First Secretary for seven months, trying both to
convince the Soviets that he was in control of events, whilst also trying
to convince his people that the Prague Spring had achieved something,
and that the Czechoslovaks had more freedoms than other Eastern

Bloc citizens. However, the Kremlin decided that Dubček was no longer in control and forced him out of the leadership.

Dubček's role in 1968 is sometimes misunderstood. He did not initiate the Prague Spring. Rather he responded to popular pressure, sometimes unwillingly, and when Soviet control of Czechoslovakia was threatened, he gave in to Soviet demands. One historian wrote:

> 1 In retrospect, it can be seen that Dubček's espousal of liberal causes in 1968 was more connected with his attempts to introduce a federal structure in Czechoslovakia and to provide an economic impetus for the system, than with a desire to introduce parliamentary democracy. Nor
> 5 was Dubček a strong champion of the intellectuals. He merely perceived the intellectuals as an important element in the country's revival ... his commitment to 'Communism with a human face' was sincere, his devotion to the socialist cause and to the Soviet Union was not in doubt.
> (Olga Narkiewicz, *Petrification and Progress: Communist Leaders in Eastern Europe 1956-1988*, Harvester Wheatsheaf 1990.)

Dubček later issued his own defence of the Prague Spring, in an interview in 1988:

> 1 Our programme [in 1968] was spontaneously received with unprecedented enthusiasm by the whole party and the entire people ... Our people - our workers, farmers and intellectuals - were supporting and defending their party, they were joining it without being called on to do
> 5 so ... Would the Czechoslovak people have worked in the factories, cooperatives, offices and other institutions with a zeal and enthusiasm not recalled by anyone before or since had there been a 'counter-revolutionary situation threatening a reversal back to capitalism?' ... Even though the revival process lasted barely nine months, the annual
> 10 economic results by far exceeded earlier growth as well as the average annual growth rate of the Czechoslovak national income for 1969-1986. Is that how people behave in times of chaos and disruption of society? Who will believe that?

An anti-Soviet cartoon showing the change in the USSRs attitude towards Czechoslovakia between 1945 and 1968

Whatever his real motives at the time, Dubček probably miscalculated. He knew that the Soviet leadership itself was divided on Czechoslovakia, and the fact that the USSR first threatened invasion in March and then did nothing for five months may have led him to believe that it might not happen.

Brezhnev's was probably the determining voice in the events of 1968-9. His behaviour suggested that he might concede a measure of economic change, but political concessions were another matter. In Brezhnev's eyes, the crime of the Czechoslovak reformers was to link economic and political reform. Dubček's vision of a Communist Party having to compete with democratic parties for people's votes was simply not acceptable to the Soviets in 1968, just as it had not been acceptable in Hungary in 1956, although there were echoes of both Nagy and Dubček in Gorbachev's reforms in the USSR in the 1980s.

It took some time to secure Czechoslovakia safely within the Soviet fold, although there was not the bloodshed which had marked the Hungarian Rising. Apart from Dubček's demotion, there were major purges in 1970. Almost a third of Party members were dismissed or resigned voluntarily. Nearly 3,000 journalists and professors were dismissed. Over 100,000 Czechoslovaks left the country. In January 1969 a student, Jan Palach, gained international publicity by burning himself to death in Prague's Wenceslas Square in protest at events in Czechoslovakia.

The USSR issued the Brezhnev Doctrine in September 1968: the USSR reserved the right to intervene in the internal affairs of other Socialist states if Socialism were perceived as being under threat. Czechoslovakia was forced to agree to the 'temporary' stationing of Soviet troops within its borders. A Treaty of Friendship in 1970 marked a common determination by Czechoslovakia and the USSR to defend Socialism. The Soviet version of events - that the Czechoslovakian leadership had appealed for Soviet intervention in order to preempt a counter-revolutionary coup - was officially adopted in Czechoslovakia.

4 Crisis in Poland

> **KEY ISSUE** What led to the rise of *Solidarity* in Poland, what was its significance, and how did the Polish regime respond?

a) The Rise of Solidarity

1968 reinforced the message of 1956: major reforms were suspect throughout the Eastern Bloc, and the USSR was determined not to tolerate any weakening of 'Socialist unity'. Only when the Soviets themselves seriously considered reform in the 1980s did the prospect of reform in Eastern Bloc states also become feasible.

These lessons were not lost on the Polish leadership, which helped its allies suppress the Prague Spring in 1968. Yet a decade later it faced its own crisis. This crisis was not caused by reform-minded Communists and their allies but arose out of workers' discontent, which had periodically resurfaced ever since the early 1950s. The crisis in 1980 began in typical fashion: price rises, followed by strikes. Gdansk was the focus: workers in the *Lenin* shipyard went on strike, led by Lech Walesa. He called for solidarity amongst the workers and the shipyard was occupied. Strike committees demanded independent unions.

The Government was unsure of how to respond. Gierek offered economic reforms and negotiations led to an agreement in August 1980 between the Government and workers on *Solidarity*. This was to be a self-governing trade union, the first independent one in the Communist world. It was also the first mass non-Party and non-official organisation in the Eastern Bloc. The Polish Communists signed the agreement because they believed that the country was on the verge of social unrest and a general strike. The USSR organised manoeuvres along Poland's borders, probably as a warning to the Polish Government not to concede too much.

Adam Michnik, a *Solidarity* adviser, later recalled the significance of the agreement, which served as a beacon of hope to many non-Communists everywhere: 'In 1980 the totalitarian state gave in and

Striking workers at a church service at the *Lenin* shipyard, 1980

BIOGRAPHY: LECH WALESA (1943-)

The son of a carpenter, Walesa became an electrician in the Gdansk shipyards and was frequently in trouble with the authorities for organising strikes. He was on the strike committee at the *Lenin* shipyard during the 1970 riots in which many workers died. Walesa learned the lesson from those events that, rather than take the police on in the streets, the workers' best weapon was the 'occupation strike': that is, they should sit tight in the factories and passively resist until the authorities negotiated. Walesa declared: 'A wall cannot be demolished with butts of the head. We must move slowly, step by step, otherwise the wall remains untouched and we break our heads.'

Walesa came to national prominence in 1980 when he coordinated the *Lenin* shipyard strike movement into an organised and powerful force. He negotiated with the Government for the right to form independent unions. Whilst not an intellectual, Walesa was patriotic, deeply Catholic, and a believer in patience when necessary. Later he was to say of himself: 'Who is this fellow on account of whom soldiers are not allowed to take their boots off even when they sleep?'

Walesa was appointed chairman of *Solidarity*, and after it was banned he was detained for 11 months in 1981-82. When awarded the Nobel Peace Prize, he donated it to social welfare. Walesa was elected to the presidency in 1990 but failed to increase presidential power over parliament, and he was defeated in the 1995 presidential elections.

Walesa was not interested in Western-style capitalism, believing that independent unions were the best guarantee of democracy: 'We don't want to go back to capitalism or copy Western models. We live in Poland and must find Polish solutions. Socialism isn't a bad system. Let it remain - as long as it's controlled.'

---

signed an agreement which allowed for the existence of the first legal and independent institutions of postwar Polish political life. They lasted but a short time; long enough, however, to convince everyone that after December 1981 it was not possible to speak again about "socialism with a human face." What remains is communism with its teeth knocked out.'

Jacek Kuron, adviser to Walesa, declared in December 1980:

> 1 [We] build up this pluralist structure in stages and gradually dismantle totalitarianism, step by step. Very slowly. The goals of the government and of the democratic movement are completely opposite. But the struggle between the two tendencies, the totalitarian and the democ-
> 5 ratic one, is to be fought exclusively by peaceful means.

After suffering a heart attack, Gierek was replaced by Stanislaw Kania, who decided that the agreement with *Solidarity* applied only to Gdansk. When this news broke workers in other regions went on strike. *Solidarity* suffered harassment after its official recognition, but the membership held firm and the Government backed down from confrontation. In February 1981 General Wojciek Jaruzelski was appointed Prime Minister. In July almost the entire Central Committee was replaced, along with many functionaries lower down. Although moderation appeared to have won the day and the Party had officially committed itself to reform, progress was slow because there were still many in the Party opposed to giving concessions to *Solidarity*.

Walesa chaired *Solidarity*'s National Coordination Committee, and branches sprang up across Poland. The organisation declared its willingness to recognise the leading role of the Party and officially renounced any idea of overthrowing the regime or breaking with the USSR. However, *Solidarity* was a large and diffuse organisation, and some members were impatient to exert more pressure on the Government. In September 1981 the editor of a pro-*Solidarity* newspaper wrote that 'We are now in what seems to be a dead end. The economy and state are disintegrating ... It seems that waiting to see what the authorities do and negotiating has proved ineffective. *Solidarity* is slowly losing points. It is disappointing members.' *Solidarity* was difficult to control, and members disagreed about the extent to which *Solidarity* should remain a trade union or emphasise political activity. Its programme was certainly far-reaching, as this extract from February 1981 shows:

1   We were born of the protest against wrongs, humiliation, and injustice. We are an independent, self-governing labour union of the working people from all regions and all trades. We defend the rights, dignity, and interests of the entire labour world.

5   We want to mould life in our country in keeping with the ideals of patriotism, social justice, and civil democracy. As a labour union we do not intend to take over the job of the state apparatus of power. What we want to do is to represent the working people's interests before the apparatus ... The principle of equality makes it obvious that total

10 democracy must be observed in public life ... We will also demand the elimination of curbs on the right to form associations, of curbs that stem from censorship, and especially of those that ... result from manipulation in order to defend the current interests of the governing teams ...

The economic reform should shape in a new way the structure and

15 functioning of the central planning done by the main centres of command, the socialised enterprises, and the other elements of the economic system. Central planning should be deprived of its prescriptive and command characteristics ... The central distribution of raw materials and other means of production should be restricted and

20 purposefully eliminated. The work of the enterprise should be based on self-financing ...

Making the socialised enterprises independent makes it possible and even necessary to establish *authentic workers' self-government* ... *Solidarity*

BIOGRAPHY: WOJCIEK JARUZELSKI (1923-)

Jaruzelski was described in 1981 by the *Sunday Times* as a 'Polish aristocrat, one of the few remaining in today's rather proletarian society.' He was actually born into the gentry class, but his family was deported to the USSR after the Soviet annexation of Eastern Poland in 1939. He joined the Polish Army raised within the USSR, then joined the Party in 1947. He became the youngest general in the Polish army, held a series of political and military posts, and became Chief of the General Staff in 1965. Jaruzelski was elected to the Politburo in 1971 and became Prime Minister in 1981. He became president in 1989 but was succeeded by Lech Walesa in the following year.

Jaruzelski presided over the period in which Communist authority in Poland slowly crumbled.

---

is the main guarantee for the process of renewal. There is no other
25 social force in Poland that would be able to replace *Solidarity* in that job
… Either *Solidarity* transforms its social environment, or the present
system will impose its norms and goals, will paralyse our efforts, and in
the end, will swallow us up, annihilating our hopes for a rebirth.

There is no turning back from the path we have chosen. We can only
30 go forward towards the complete renewal of the country.

b) Jaruzelski and Martial Law

In October 1981 Kania was removed. Jaruzelski, already Prime Minister, became Party leader. He tried to reduce *Solidarity*'s influence by proposing that it should be but one of seven organisations to be represented in a 'Front for National Cooperation'. Such a step would have helped to maintain the Party's hold on power, and the proposal was rejected by *Solidarity*. Jaruzelski responded by abandoning compromise and declaring a state of martial law in December 1981. He was pressured by Moscow and hardliners in the Party, and was faced with the real threat of Soviet military intervention. However, the situation was very different from Hungary in 1956 or Czechoslovakia in 1968. The Soviets did not refer to the Brezhnev Doctrine, with its 'right' of intervention: the Party was still in control, and the Soviets were reluctant to send in troops, because given the long history of Polish-Soviet confrontation, massive resistance was likely, and it would have effectively ended Soviet attempts to reopen *détente* with the West, at a time when Western opinion was already very hostile to the USSR over its invasion of Afghanistan in 1979.

Jaruzelski's radio declaration of martial law on 13 December 1981 pulled few punches:

1 Our country is on the edge of the abyss. Achievements of many generations, raised from the ashes, are collapsing into ruin. State structures no
longer function. New blows are struck each day at our flickering
economy. Living conditions are burdening people more and more ...
5 Chaos and demoralisation have reached the level of defeat ... Now, not
days but hours separate us from a nationwide catastrophe ... We must
bind the hands of the adventurers before they push the country into
civil war ...

I declare that today the Army Council of National Salvation has been
10 constituted ... not as a substitute for the Constitutional government. Its
only task is to protect law in the country, to guarantee reestablishment
of order and discipline ...

In the name of national interests, a group of people threatening the
safety of the country has been interned. The extremists of *Solidarity* are
15 included in this group ...

Despite all the failures and mistakes we made, the Party is still the
leading and creative force in the process of changes to fulfil its mission
... We shall protect universal values of socialism, enriching it with our
national elements and tradition ...
20 Poles, brothers and sisters: I address all of you as a soldier who
remembers well the cruelty of war. Let's not allow a drop of Polish
blood to flow in this tormented country which has experienced so
many defeats and suffering. Let's restrain the phantom of civil war, let's
not erect barricades where a bridge is needed ...
25 I turn to all citizens. The hour of hard trial has come. We must meet

A *Solidarity* press conference, 1981

this challenge, prove that we are worthy of Poland.

Fellow countrymen, before the whole world I want to repeat these immortal words: Poland is not yet lost as long as we live.

Jaruzelski created a Military Council of National Salvation and had the *Solidarity* leaders arrested. Trade union activity was suspended. However, *Solidarity* was not completely checked: although arrests were made, strikes continued, and the strikers were supported by the Church. *Solidarity*, which boasted about nine million members in 1980, continued to operate underground after its formal banning in 1982. It published hundreds of underground books and was an inspiration to radical reformers in other Eastern Bloc states. Its existence was guaranteed by continuing economic problems, and unrest followed the Government's decision in 1982 to raise prices again by 76 per cent.

5 Assessment

> **KEY ISSUE** Why were the challenges to Communist rule compara-
> tively unsuccessful before 1989?

Solidarity was to reemerge to play a major role in the downfall of Communism in Poland. The continued existence of a large-scale opposition movement, combined with the absence of direct Soviet intervention and the fact that the bulk of the Polish opposition came from outside the Party, were the principal differences between the Polish crisis and the dramatic events in Hungary and Czechoslovakia in 1956 and 1968. However, none of the movements for fundamental change in Eastern Bloc countries succeeded in significantly changing the nature of the regimes in the years between 1948 and 1989. The reasons for this were varied, but there were common strands. It was very difficult in an authoritarian state to form organised opposition: the regimes, with their monopoly of information and strong security apparatuses, could isolate individual dissidents. Organised opposition could sometimes develop. as it did in Poland, but it was rare. There were individual opinions and even sometimes groups in favour of limited reform in authoritarian societies. Some reformers were seeking economic changes which would modify the command economies, and were usually aimed at introducing features of a market economy which would make industry more responsive to supply and demand and would improve quality and productivity. Some of the regimes – notably Hungary – and the USSR itself were prepared to tolerate a limited amount of economic debate. However, if the debate challenged the essential notion of the state-run economy, or even more threatening, spilled over into demands for political reform, debate was stifled. In any case, most citizens had no political outlet for dissent;

and most Party members either believed implicitly in the system or had too much of a stake in it to want reform, whilst bureaucracy bred its own resistance to change. The Hungarian and Czechoslovakian radicals learned in 1956 and 1968 the dangers of proposing significant changes which threatened the apparent unity of the Eastern Bloc. Although *Solidarity* was eventually victorious in Poland, it was a long struggle, and Soviet intervention was narrowly averted. Ultimately the Eastern Bloc regimes were to crumble within a few months of each other in 1989 as the pressure for radical change grew throughout Eastern and Central Europe. This was due to a combination of factors, not least of which was the declared reluctance of the USSR to continue supporting hardline regimes against pressure for democratic change and economic liberalisation. How that pressure developed rapidly is the theme of the next chapter.

Making notes on 'Revolt'

This chapter focuses on challenges to Communist regimes in Hungary, Czechoslovakia and Poland. In each case you are seeking not just information about what happened, but answers to these questions: why did the challenges occur? Did the challenges originate inside or outside the Party? What was the Soviet response? Why did the challenges in Hungary and Czechoslovakia fail? How did the Polish regime manage the crisis? What were the short- and long-term consequences of these challenges? What comparisons and contrasts can be made between events in the three countries?

Answering structured questions and essay questions on 'Revolt'

Material from this chapter will probably be used to answer questions which focus either on specific crises in Hungary, Czechoslovakia or Poland, or questions may ask you to make a comparison between events in two or more of these countries. However, the chapter will also provide useful material for many other questions to do with the nature of political control, opposition and relationships with the USSR for most of the period covered by this book. When answering questions on specific crises, you should be prepared to consider long-term and short-term causes and consequences: why the crises occurred; how they were dealt with; what were the results both for the countries concerned and possibly the Eastern Bloc as a whole. Dealing with these aspects will be more important than outlining the actual events, although of course you must be able to put forward your arguments in an historical context.

A typical example of the 'individual' question is:

1. 'Why, and with what consequences, did the movement for reform in Czechoslovakia fail in 1968?'

An example of the 'comparison' question is:

2. 'To what extent were the motives for Soviet intervention in Hungary in 1956 similar to those in Czechoslovakia in 1968?'

Essay number 1 has a fairly narrow focus, requiring a reasonably detailed knowledge of the events and circumstances of 1968. The key words are 'Why' and 'With what consequences'. Your introduction should analyse the question, and is also likely to establish the context of the Prague Spring. You should then examine what the reformers both inside and outside the Party were trying to achieve. Dubček's role should be analysed, and of course the reasons for the Soviet invasion and its effects.

'Consequences' needs careful treatment. The obvious answer to the first part is to emphasise that the defeat of the Prague Spring effectively put the hardliners back into power, and they determinedly resisted reform for as long as possible, that is until the late 1980s. You should consider both the short-term and the longer-term consequences, and decide how much weight to give to each. You should also refer to the international context - for example the fact that the events of 1968 reinforced Cold War suspicions and led to the Brezhnev Doctrine and a renewed emphasis upon Socialist solidarity. However, you should not dwell too much on the international consequences at the expense of the internal ones.

The key words in essay number 2 are 'To what extent', 'motives' and 'similar'. In each case your answer will need to briefly establish the context of revolt in 1956 Hungary and 1968 Czechoslovakia, examining the role of reformers inside and outside the Party, their aims, the relationships of the regimes with the USSR, the international context of the Cold War, and Soviet and Warsaw Pact concerns about the unity of the Eastern Bloc and the possible consequences of a radically different regime in either country for the region and international politics as a whole. You are almost certainly likely to conclude that Soviet motives were to a large extent similar in both instances; but a good answer will also highlight possible differences in the situation between the two countries, due to both circumstances and the individuals involved.

1. Hungarian Demands in 1956

Read carefully the demands of the workers' council in 1956 on page 79. Answer the following questions:

a) Using your own knowledge, explain what had happened in Hungary to prompt this declaration. (4 marks)
b) Summarise the demands made by the authors of this declaration. (4 marks)
c) Comment on the language and tone of this declaration. (4 marks)
d) Using your own knowledge, explain the extent to which the demands in this declaration were met. (4 marks)
e) How useful is this source as evidence of discontent with the Communist regime in Hungary? (4 marks)

2. Imre Nagy's Broadcast During the Hungarian Rising

Study carefully the extract from Nagy's radio broadcast on pages 79-80 and answer the following questions:

a) Using your own knowledge, outline the part played by Nagy in Hungarian politics prior to this broadcast. (4 marks)
b) What explanation does Nagy give for this 'tragic fratricidal fight'? (5 marks)
c) Compare the language and tone of this source with that of the workers' council declaration on page 79. (5 marks)
d) Using this source, and your own knowledge, comment on the accuracy of Nagy's interpretation of events. (6 marks)

3. The Action Programme of 1968

Read carefully the extract from the 1968 Action Plan of the Czechoslovakian Party on page 85. Answer the following questions:

a) Using your own knowledge, explain the background to this Programme (4 marks)
b) Summarise the message of the Programme and explain in what ways it was radical. (5 marks)
c) Compare the tone of this Programme with that of the source on page 83. How do you account for the differences? (6 marks)
d) What is the reliability of this source as evidence of the attitudes of the Czechoslovak reformers in 1968? (5 marks)

4. Solidarity's Programme

Study carefully the extract from the *Solidarity* programme of 1981 on pages 91-2. Answer the following questions:

a) What events had led to the issuing of this Programme? (5 marks)

b) What political and economic reforms did *Solidarity* champion in this Programme? (6 marks)
c) How radical were *Solidarity's* demands? (4 marks)
d) Were *Solidarity's* claims to be 'the main guarantee' (line 24) of the success of reform justified? (5 marks)

5. Martial Law

Read carefully the extract from Jaruzelski's declaration of Martial Law on pages 93-94. Answer the following questions:

a) Using the extract and your own knowledge, explain why this declaration was made. (5 marks)
b) How accurate was Jaruzelski's analysis of the crisis? (5 marks)
c) Comment on the techniques used by Jaruzelski in this declaration to win support. (5 marks)
d) To what extent were the aims of the declaration achieved? (5 marks)

Summary Diagram

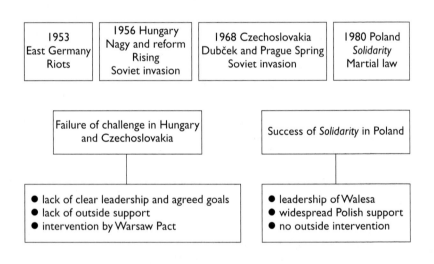

7 Collapse

POINTS TO CONSIDER

This chapter will focus upon the pressures which led to the collapse of the Communist regimes of Central and Eastern Europe in the late 1980s. Your aim on first reading the chapter should be to establish the sequence of events which led to the revolutions, their causes, and the relationship, if any, between the events in the various countries in order to establish an overall picture of the transition from Communist to post-Communist rule.

1 Pressures For Change

KEY ISSUE What political, social and economic pressures lay behind the collapse of Communist regimes at the end of the 1980s?

By the late 1980s many people anticipated major economic or political changes in the Eastern Bloc. Nevertheless when changes came, many, including some of the political leaders themselves, were surprised by their speed. The regimes reacted in a variety of ways, but none of the old generation of leaders survived for long. Some held out against change for longer than others.

Possibly the most crucial factor in all of the events of the late 1980s was the attitude of the USSR. Mikhail Gorbachev had come to power in 1985 with his own domestic agenda: he wanted to reform the USSR economically and politically, and his policies of *glasnost*, or openness, and *perestroika*, or restructuring, were crucial to the process. Gorbachev did not have a consistent plan for reform and faced considerable apathy and resistance from his own people. However, the very fact that a Soviet leader was bent on dismantling Stalinism was bound to have an impact in the Soviet-dominated Eastern Bloc; and once it was clear that the USSR was not going to shore up reactionary regimes elsewhere, a green light was given for resistance to those regimes from their subjects. Certainly the possibility of another 1956 or 1968 no longer existed. Some of the regimes tried to adapt and save themselves. They failed principally because none of them had succeeded in maintaining a consistent rise in living standards, which alone might have secured the loyalty of people who were increasingly aware that Socialist Europe was not competing with the more advanced societies of Western Europe, which also allowed its people considerably more personal freedom.

2 The Crisis of Communism

> **KEY ISSUE** How and why did the Communist regimes of Central and Eastern Europe disintegrate?

a) Poland: The Triumph of Solidarity

Whilst no one group or individual took the lead in dismantling Communism, in some respects Poland was the key. It alone of the Eastern Bloc states contained a large, relatively organised opposition group, *Solidarity*, albeit one which operated underground after 1980-1. Poland was also the first Eastern Bloc country for 40 years to produce a Government not controlled by the Communists.

Although *Solidarity* had been driven underground, the Communists' hold on Poland was increasingly insecure. There was a purge within the Party, but membership declined and the Party's own survey in 1987 revealed that only a quarter of the membership was playing an active role. Although Jaruzelski lifted martial law in 1983, other repressive laws remained in force. *Solidarity* urged voters to boycott local elections in 1984, and the turnout was so low that many elections had to be re-fought to meet electoral requirements. This was an unusual state of affairs in one-party states which prided themselves on their ability to mobilise voters to give their stamp of authority to regimes. Jaruzelski began reforms probably in response to Gorbachev's policies in the USSR, and he may have hoped for the popular mandate for his rule that had been singularly lacking thus far. However, real incomes were falling and the Government failed to win enough support in a referendum in 1987 on introducing an austerity package. Further price increases in 1988 fomented more strikes.

The Polish Government took an important decision in August 1988 to compromise with what it termed the 'constructive opposition'. The following January it decided to legalise *Solidarity*, introduce political pluralism, and hold 'Round Table' negotiations with *Solidarity* and the Church. *Solidarity* was free to operate openly with its own newspapers and exposure on radio and television. Its triumph was an inspiration to reformers elsewhere; and like the breaching of the Berlin Wall, it was to symbolise the ending of the postwar Socialist order in Eastern and Central Europe. The following elections in June 1989 helped to precipitate political revolution in neighbouring Eastern Bloc states.

In the first round of the elections *Solidarity* won all but one of the 35 per cent of the parliamentary seats open to opposition candidates. It won over 90 per cent of the Senate seats. Despite having many more resources, the Communists won only 38 per cent of the seats in the *Sejm*, or parliament. Walesa declared: 'This is the beginning of democracy and a free Poland.' In the second round *Solidarity* won all the 161 *Sejm* seats it contested and 99 out of 100 Senate seats.

Jaruzelski accepted reality. Having just narrowly been elected by Parliament as President, he invited *Solidarity* to join a coalition Government and resigned the party leadership. *Solidarity* refused the invitation, partly because of its strength and because of unhappy memories of coalitions with Communists. Jaruzelski admitted defeat and invited Tadeusz Mazowiecki, editor of the *Solidarity* newspaper, to form a Government. It contained 11 *Solidarity* members and representatives of other parties, although Communists still controlled the military and internal defence forces. The Communists virtually collapsed as an organised group and reconstituted themselves as a Social Democratic Party. Communist control over the police and army was finally removed in 1990.

Of particular significance was the fact that the USSR allowed these events to happen. Soviet inaction sent a clear signal to the Eastern Bloc that the USSR had abandoned former Communist allies. Members of Gorbachev's Government spoke approvingly of the Poles following the 'Sinatra Doctrine' or 'My Way'.

b) Hungary: Disintegration

As in Poland, Hungarian Communists were compromised by their inability to sustain economic growth. Kádár admitted at the Party Congress in 1985 that living standards had fallen and that foreign debts were mounting. A domestic opposition emerged, taking its lead from Gorbachev's reforms in the USSR. In September 1987 the Hungarian Democratic Forum (HDF) was formed, followed by the Alliance of Young Democrats (FIDESZ) and other parties. The Communists tried to respond. Kádár was sacked, along with some hardline colleagues, in May 1988. Kádár had won tacit consent from the Soviets for economic reform. However, sustained economic reform had proved impossible without the genuine political reform to accompany it, and Kádár had not been prepared to tolerate that. Like other leaders brought up in the Stalinist system, he might show limited flexibility but would do nothing to challenge the fundamentals of the system which he had inherited.

Kádár's successor as leader was the 57 year-old Karoly Grósz, hardly a liberal. He set up a commission which reached the significant conclusion that the 1956 Rising had been a popular event and not a counterrevolution. When the Party accepted this judgement in February 1989, it effectively destroyed the basis of its own legitimacy, since its policies after 1956 had been based on the claim that it was protecting Hungary from counterrevolution. The key to the ending of Communist control was the Party's acceptance of multi-party politics. The old system began to disintegrate of its own accord, before it was even pushed from outside. 'New' Communists permitted capitalism and political competition, and it was a relatively peaceful process.

The Communists announced in March 1989 that they were

prepared to join a coalition government. Talks were begun with an alliance of opposition parties known as the Opposition Round Table. Whilst the talks were in progress, the Government decided to allow thousands of East Germans, supposedly holidaying in Hungary, to cross the border into Austria. This action sparked off a chain reaction in East Germany leading to the breaching of the Berlin Wall and the reunification of Germany. In September the Hungarian Government dismantled all its border barriers.

In October 1989 the reformers within the Communist Party triumphed at an Extraordinary Congress and the Party's name was changed to the Hungarian Socialist Party (HSP). A rump of old Communists remained outside, but several Communist organisations were dismantled. When a referendum on the constitution was held in November, the opposition parties were divided, but even so the HSP did badly, proof that the Communists' attempts to reform themselves had failed to convince the electorate. The parliamentary elections of March and April 1990 were among the first completely free elections in the Eastern Bloc. There was not a decisive result, but the HDF formed a coalition with two other parties, Hungary's first non-Communist Government since the 1940s. The HSP secured only 8 per cent of the vote.

c) Czechoslovakia: The Ghosts of 1968

Events in Czechoslovakia took a different turn. There was already the beginnings of an organised opposition well before the 1980s: in 1977 a group called Charter 77 had been formed to 'resist the lie' of 1968 and to monitor human rights. It had been periodically persecuted, and the Party tried to hold out against reform: unlike Hungary, the end of Communism in Czechoslovakia was not in part due to reformers opening the floodgates of reform from within the Party, but due to the fact that the Party could not compete with opposition from outside its own ranks and had no popular support.

Husák had proved a hardline leader and out of sympathy with Gorbachev. In 1987 he was replaced by another conservative, Miloš Jakeš. Popular disaffection with the progress of change was marked by large anti-Government demonstrations in 1989. The Government arrested Václav Havel, a prominent playwright and dissident, whose satirical writings on Communism had been banned since 1969. But there were growing contacts with dissident groups in Poland and Hungary, and then the breaching of the Berlin Wall in November 1989 provided a flashpoint. It persuaded some Communists to stage a coup against their own hardline leadership. Events were complicated by demonstrations possibly provoked by Soviet agents trying to produce a Government crisis and pave the way for a pro-reform Communist regime. The demonstrations were relatively restrained, and hence the events became known as the Velvet Revolution. Whilst Jakeš' regime hesitated, a group of opponents formed Civic Forum to coordinate the campaign for an end to Communist rule. A parallel organisation called Public Against Violence was set up in Slovakia.

In a desperate change of tactics, the Communist leadership resigned en bloc, and a new Communist Government was appointed under the more moderate Ladislav Adamec. Failure to win opposition approval soon led to a new Government of National Understanding under the younger Communist Marián Čalfa. His Government included a majority of non-Communists. Čalfa left the Party and joined Public against Violence, whilst Husák resigned the presidency. Change finally came quickly: there were promises of free elections and market reforms, and Havel was appointed President by the Assembly in December 1989. When the promised elections were finally held in June 1990, the situation was complicated by the existence of a Federal Assembly and separate Republican governments granted to the Czech lands and Slovakia in 1989. Civic Forum and Public Against Violence together won a clear majority in the Federal Assembly and the Czech National Council, although with 13 per cent of the votes in both Republics, the Communists did better than in any other Eastern Bloc country at this time.

d) The End of the Wall and the GDR

The collapse of Communism was perhaps most dramatically illustrated in East Germany, if only because of the symbolic as well as the physical importance of the breaching of the Berlin Wall. The East German regime was one of those that held out longest against real change. As late as mid-1989 the old order seemed intact: the local elections of May 1989 were manipulated in the usual fashion, and the Socialist Unity Party achieved its customary 98 per cent of the vote, its candidates being the only ones allowed to stand.

However, there were serious undercurrents of unrest emerging. East Germans knew better than ever that they were worse off than their counterparts in the West. Honecker began to face dissent within the Party. He increasingly relied upon a few advisers and acted alone in foreign policy. He allowed no debate about policy. Once it became clear that the USSR would not intervene to maintain the existing regime, its authority quickly crumbled, although Honecker was slow to appreciate the fact. He was incapacitated for much of 1989 by serious illness, and often government seemed to come to a standstill.

Hungary was the key. East German citizens had been agitating since March 1989 for the right to travel outside the Eastern Bloc, Leipzig being the venue for the first major demonstration. In September 25,000 East Germans supposedly 'holidaying' in Hungary succeeded in crossing the border into Austria and freedom. The GDR's Government made no serious attempt to close this route, and new political groups began to form at home. The first was 'New Forum', followed by 'Democracy Now' and others. Some of Honecker's colleagues were frustrated by his inability to offer anything except 'a strategic concept of continuity and renewal.' The real push for change came from Gorbachev on a visit to East Berlin on 6 October, ironically the fortieth anniversary of the founding of the GDR. Gorbachev uttered the cryptic warning, 'Those who delay are punished by life.' Honecker replied, 'Those who are declared dead usually live a long time,' revealing either misplaced optimism or complacency.

Following Gorbachev's visit, demonstrations spread across the GDR. The regime's dilemma was that it was increasingly difficult to contain pressure for change, but if it opened the borders the youngest and most vigorous elements of the population would almost certainly leave. 7 out of the 23 members of the Politburo plotted against Honecker. He was persuaded at a Politburo meeting to resign, having been told that there might otherwise be a national uprising, and Gorbachev had announced that he could no longer be relied upon by the GDR leadership to keep it in power. Gorbachev told Egon Krenz, Honecker's successor:

1   If [Honecker] had, on his own initiative, introduced basic policy
    correctives two or three years ago, then such losses and difficulties
    would have been neither necessary nor possible. Comrade Erich
    Honecker obviously considered himself to be Number One in
5   Socialism, perhaps even in the whole world. He no longer saw clearly
    what was really going on.

Krenz replied:

    Suddenly Honecker found himself confronted with a young, dynamic
    leader [Gorbachev], who tackled new questions in a very
    unconventional way. Until this time he had seen himself in this role.
    Gradually he lost his sense of reality.

Krenz was approved by Moscow, but he was far from being a popular choice, particularly since he was in charge of the notorious *Stasi*. As a representative of the old regime he believed that the Communists could stay in control if there were some changes of personnel and a few concessions to the popular mood. But the demonstrations continued. On 9 November 1989 came the momentous announcement that the borders with both West Berlin and the West German state would be opened. That night the Berlin Wall was breached in an atmosphere of jubilation. Two million East Germans visited the West over the subsequent weekend. These events caused the cynical Krenz leadership to lose its nerve, realising that moderate concessions were no longer enough. Krenz resigned, to be replaced by a reformist Communist Government with Gregor Gysi Chairman of the Party of Democratic Socialism (the old Socialist Unity Party) and Hans Modrow as Prime Minister. The Party was renamed again in February 1990 as the Party of Democratic Socialism (PDS). Modrow brought 11 non-Communists into the Government and announced plans for a market economy and criminal charges against Honecker.

Negotiations soon began for the reunification of Germany. Before that, the first free elections in East Germany were held in March 1990. The more established West German parties competed in the election and dominated it, a foretaste of the dominant influence the West was to have over future events. The first and last democratically elected GDR Government was formed on 9 April, a coalition of Conservatives, Social Democrats and Liberals. Thereafter the preoccupation was unification.

e) Bulgaria: The Fall of Zhivkov

Bulgaria was another example of a Communist regime which reacted too slowly and too late to the changing conditions of the 1980s to save itself. In 1987 Zhivkov announced the 'July Concept', promising liberal reforms, partly in response to an economic downturn and partly in response to developments in Gorbachev's USSR. The rate of economic growth fell from over 5 per cent in 1986 to 0.4 per cent by 1989, while foreign debts mounted. Bulgaria was paying the price for an antiquated industrial structure and a lack of substantial reform in the past. In 1988 enterprises were allowed to issue their own stocks or bonds. However, whilst the regime was responding with its own version of restructuring, it was not in favour of *glasnost* or 'openness'. Critics who demanded more reforms were sacked or arrested, and the regime insisted that, although opposition movements were forming, there could be no attack on the principles of Socialism. In October 1989 a reform demonstration in Sofia was broken up in a blaze of world publicity. The regime had already courted criticism by miscalculating in its Turkish policy. In May 1989 Turkish demonstrators had been met with violence. Zhivkov challenged the Turkish Government to open its borders. The Government called his bluff, opened the border, and 300,000 Bulgarian Turks fled across. The exodus was so unmanageable that Turkey had to close the border again, but the ethnic Turks had made their preferences clear.

With stability increasingly threatened, an anti-Zhivkov conspiracy in the Party hierarchy got the support of the military. On the day after the Berlin Wall was breached, the Central Committee deposed Zhivkov. It was a coup organised from within the Party, without popular participation, and in this respect the Bulgarian revolution was different from some of the others. Because the regime had not been notably unpopular, popular participation in events developed after the Revolution rather than being a principal cause of it. The new leader, Peter Mladenov, sacked leading Zhivkovites and promised democratic elections and economic restructuring leading to a dismantling of the economy. The Communists renamed themselves the Bulgarian Socialist party (BSP) and reformed themselves in response to the formation of opposition groups, which allied themselves in the Union of Democratic Forces (UDF).

f) Romania: Revolution Against Ceauşescu

Romania was the slowest of the Eastern Bloc countries to experience change, because of its relatively slow rate of development and the stranglehold over the country which Ceauşescu's regime had maintained. Overt opposition was dangerous and rare. Outbreaks of unrest amongst miners in the late 1970s and early 1980s, and violent demonstrations amongst students in the industrial town of Brasov in 1987, were vigorously suppressed. The regime seemed unruffled by the dramatic changes facing other Eastern Bloc regimes in the late 1980s. But Ceauşescu was increasingly isolated and could expect no aid from the Soviets or elsewhere.

In 1987 a secret 'National Salvation Front' organisation circulated a document calling for Ceauşescu's removal. December 1987 saw Ceauşescu reelected head of the Party but also dramatic events in Transylvania. As a result of their ill-treatment, thousands of ethnic Hungarians had been fleeing into Hungary. The authorities tried to deport one of the focal points of resistance, a popular Hungarian priest, László Tökés, from Timosoara. Romanians and Hungarians demonstrated in support of him. A state of emergency was declared in Timosoara, and the *Securitate* killed 71 demonstrators.

Ceauşescu misread the signs. He dismissed the demonstrations as the work of 'hooligan elements' amongst Hungarian nationalists and convened a rally in Bucharest. The intention was to drum up support, a common tactic. However, Ceauşescu incensed the crowd by showing no compassion for the victims. There were disturbances and clashes with the police that evening. Ceauşescu summoned another meeting for the next day, 22 December. The crowd was hostile. When the Army sided with the people against the *Securitate*, even Ceauşescu recognised the danger. With his wife he escaped from Bucharest by helicopter. They were soon captured, summarily tried and executed on Christmas day. The National Salvation Front (NSF) declared itself openly, and those members of the *Securitate* still loyal to the old regime were hunted down and killed.

3 Disintegration

KEY ISSUE What problems confronted the post-Communist regimes and how successfully did they begin to cope with them?

In the space of a few months all the countries of the Eastern Bloc had undergone major political changes. This, along with the break-up of the USSR in 1991, was to have major implications for the whole of Eastern and Central Europe and indeed the wider world, given the context of the Cold War which had dominated international relations since the Second World War. It was a time of optimism, but new political regimes had to face great economic and social problems, meet the demands of expectant populations and establish democratic institutions in countries which had not known democracy, certainly in recent times. It was also one thing to remove the old Communist Party leaders, another to dismantle the whole administrative structure, economic system and institutions inherited from 40 years of authoritarian rule.

None of the countries found an easy path to stability. In Poland the priority was the economy, which continued to suffer from inflation, rising unemployment and falling output, whilst a new unstable party system and a complex electoral system hindered stability. Jaruzelski resigned the presidency in September 1990 and was succeeded by Walesa. Free parliamentary elections were finally held in October 1991. But *Solidarity* suffered splits over strategy; nationalist parties increased their support as uncertainty bred disillusionment; and adjustment to the post-Communist world proved painful.

Czechoslovakia also found it difficult to arrest economic decline and move to a market economy. The situation was complicated by nationalist issues: despite little evidence of widespread popular support for the break-up of the state, political rivalries led to the 'Velvet Divorce' of 1993 by which the Czech Republic and Slovakia separated. Slovakia suffered several political crises, and although the Czech Republic developed a reputation for stability, in both countries a substantial legacy of support for both Communists and right-wing movements remained.

Political life in post-Communist Hungary was complicated by disagreements between the President and parliament, and persistent economic problems of unemployment and falling output. The ineffectiveness of governments led to a big increase in support for the Socialists during the early 1990s.

East Germany found that reunification with the West, formalised in the Treaty of Unification of 31 August 1990, was only the start of its problems: politics were dominated by West German parties, unemployment grew, and disparities with the West were simply highlighted. East Germany alone of the former Eastern Bloc states tried to convert to a full-blooded market economy overnight and the results in the short term were disastrous for many citizens.

The Bulgarian and Romanian experiences were different: one of the problems in these two countries was the continued influence of former Communists. The NSF which replaced Ceauşescu in Romania, and which contained many Communists, acted in an authoritarian manner. Continued economic difficulties provoked unrest towards political opponents, whilst ethnic Hungarians felt threatened by nationalist groups. Romania certainly typified the difficulties of introducing political and economic reform into a country without democratic traditions and which had been subject for many years to propaganda and repression. Political uncertainty and argument in Bulgaria also hindered reform there, and when elections were held in October 1991 the former Communists received substantial support, and they were to receive an absolute majority in 1994, perhaps a reflection of the fact that there had been a long period of stability under the old regime.

Therefore for all the countries covered in this book, the end of Communism was fraught with difficulties as well as hope, and it would be a long time before the events of the late 1980s and beyond could be assessed from a proper perspective. Certainly Eastern and Central Europe entered the 1990s facing an uncertain future.

Making notes on 'Collapse'

Your aim in tackling this chapter and making notes is to understand the shorter-term reasons for the collapse of the various regimes which are the subject of this book and to examine the connections between the events throughout the region in the late 1980s. Particular factors to consider are the role of the USSR in these events and the role of the various Communist Parties - for example, to what extent did they compromise with the popular mood for change, and why were they nevertheless forced out of power, although Communist influence was not dead in some of the countries?

Answering structured questions and essay questions on 'Collapse'

Essays on the collapse of Communism in Eastern and Central Europe will fall into two categories: those concentrating on particular countries, and those covering the whole region, and possibly inviting a comparison between countries and looking for common themes.

An example of the first type is: 'How important was *Solidarity* in bringing about the eventual downfall of Communism in Poland?'

An example of the second type is: 'With reference to at least three countries, explain why the Communist regimes of Eastern and Central Europe were overthrown so quickly in the late 1980s.'

In essay number 1 the key words and phrases are 'How important' and 'bringing about the eventual downfall of Communism.' You will need to know some detail about *Solidarity*'s activities and assess the importance of *Solidarity* in galvanising popular support against the regime. Did its suppression simply delay change, and how significant was the decision to legalise *Solidarity* after its victory in the 1989 elections? Crucially, would the changes have come about anyway, given the fundamental problems facing the Polish economy, or was *Solidarity* the key factor? Do not be afraid to express a firm opinion, as long as you can produce enough evidence to make it a credible argument.

In essay number 2 the key words and phrases are 'explain why' and 'overthrown so quickly'. With 'causes' questions, it is usually a good

Summary Diagram

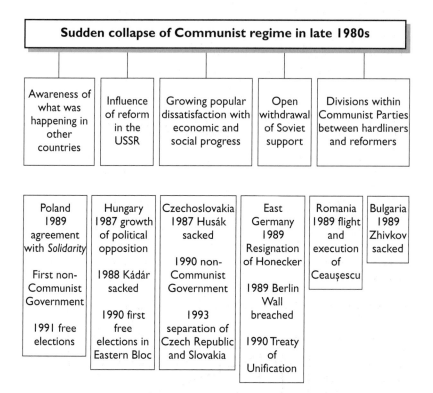

idea to separate longer-term from short-term causes. You may wish to examine the argument that the regimes had been facing potential problems for some time, particularly due to their failure to sustain economic growth, which might have won them popular support. Then you will need to explain the more short-term or immediate factors, such as the apparent withdrawal of Soviet support, divisions within the Communists' ranks, the growth of opposition movements, the cumulative effect of events in one country reacting on another. As always, whilst you must produce evidence to support your arguments, it is the sustained critical argument which will be the key to a good answer, not the ability to describe or write a narrative of events.

8 Conclusion: Eastern and Central Europe, 1945-92

POINTS TO CONSIDER

This chapter is a broad survey of the experience of 40 years of Communism in Central and Eastern Europe. Your aim in reading the chapter should be to acquire an overall understanding of the history of this period, with a particular focus on the principal trends throughout the region during this time.

In earlier chapters the Communist takeover of power in Central and Eastern Europe at the end of the Second World War was examined in detail. Also examined were the policies of the Communist regimes and the reasons for their eventual demise. From the perspective of post-Communist Europe, what had been the chief trends and issues of the previous 40 years?

The collapse of Communist regimes in the late 1980s meant a new era in the development of the region. If the breakup of the Soviet Union in 1991 is taken into account, it was also the beginning of a new era for the wider world: the crumbling of European Communism put an end to the Cold War. International problems and nuclear arsenals remained, but the period of sustained East-West tension and armed stand-off between the two Superpowers ended. The Eastern Bloc countries, integral to the Soviet defence structure, had played an important role in the Cold War, and the relaxation of international tension came as a relief to many people on both sides of the Iron Curtain. The new governments of the old Eastern Bloc countries were also relieved: high levels of defence spending had put additional strains on economies for many years.

However, euphoria generated by the radical changes of the late 1980s and early 1990s did not last. For all its lack of political freedoms, for a long time the old Eastern Bloc structure had offered some certainties such as employment and a basic state provision of services. The new governments inherited faltering economies which could not meet the popular expectation of a rising standing of living, improving social services and guaranteed employment. In the 'brave new world' of 1990s political pluralism and market economies, individuals had to fend for themselves without the all-embracing protection of the state. There were opportunities for individuals to do well but also possibilities of failure. Previous political, economic and social systems had become fossilised within what remained, even after 1953, an essentially Stalinist structure. Regimes based upon one-party authoritarian rule and a command economy had not adapted easily to new circumstances. People were not used to change and exercising individual initiative. This was compounded by the previous history of the Eastern and Central European region: here there was little tradition of democracy, popular enterprise or a capitalist culture, even before the Communists had come to power. Even the East Germans, from a more developed background, struggled after unification as the poor cousins of their West German counterparts. The prospects for political, economic and social progress in the new democracies were still murky in the first half of the 1990s.

1 What had the regimes of Central and Eastern Europe achieved in 40 years of Communist domination, and what was the nature of those regimes?

KEY ISSUE What achievements had the regimes of the Eastern Bloc managed during 40 years, and what had been the key features of the regimes?

Once Communist governments or Communist-dominated coalitions had come to power in the 1940s, they achieved a stability welcomed after the trauma of the war years and problems before 1939, although this was of less comfort to a more developed state like Czechoslovakia which had enjoyed democracy before 1939. For the Eastern Bloc as a whole, what was the price of the new stability?

Even in countries like East Germany where the Communists tolerated other parties, it was they who held the positions of importance and determined policy. One-party rule prevailed. Communist parties operated a restricted, disciplined membership in the Leninist tradition of 'democratic centralism', which meant taking orders from a small ruling group. There was no separation of powers between those who made the laws, those who governed and those who interpreted the laws in the courts. This contrasted with the Western liberal tradition, which regarded such a separation as essential if abuses of power were to be avoided.

Stability in the Eastern Bloc was also enforced through the exercise of strong Soviet influence. When the Communist monopoly of power appeared to be threatened, or Communists themselves followed an independent line, the Soviet Union issued threats or directly intervened to impose its will, albeit with the support of allies. The Hungarian Rising, the Prague Spring and the rise of *Solidarity* in Poland stand out because such events were few and far between. Reformers in these states failed to achieve their most important objectives. Political control within the Eastern Bloc was exerted through the manipulation of elections, propaganda, Communist domination of internal security, purges, indoctrination of the population (especially the young), censorship, and all the other paraphernalia of the modern totalitarian state. Those who could not be convinced by propaganda could usually be silenced through fear of the consequences of overt opposition.

The Communist regimes were not immune from internal rivalries and political infighting. In several countries, particularly in the immediate postwar years, there were bloody purges. However, in the last resort the regimes were accountable to no one (except, indirectly, to the USSR) and the winners of internal power struggles were fortified by a genuine conviction that they were constructing Socialism in the interests of their populations, particularly the working class.

Most of the first generation of postwar Communist leaders had a specific but narrow vision, that of creating political and economic systems on the Soviet model. They followed Stalin's policies. These men had endured hard political apprenticeships and were ruthless in furthering their own interests and those of their regimes. The next generation of leaders was often more able and better educated, but had to grapple with considerable problems, especially economic ones.

Did the Eastern Bloc regimes establish and maintain themselves solely by force? In East Germany, Poland and Romania there was no widespread support for Communism, and it was imposed largely by the threat or actual presence of the Red Army. There was considerable popular support for Communism in Bulgaria but, since it had been an Axis power in the Second World War, it was occupied by the Red Army anyway. In Czechoslovakia and Hungary there was considerable popular support for the Communists in the immediate postwar years, and in some quarters the Soviets were even seen as liberators. The Communists had an honourable wartime record against the occupying powers, at least after Hitler attacked the USSR. Pre-war regimes, mostly authoritarian, had presided over economic and social systems that were agriculturally-based and semi-feudal, with land and power invested in small élites, which lorded it over a poor and semi-literate peasantry. The economies, excepting Germany and Czechoslovakia, were non-industrial and backward. The prewar regimes had often been conservative, nationalistic and intolerant.

The Communist regimes swept away these old élites, and began to industrialise. Peasant populations were halved in numbers, and those left were educated. Many of the grosser inequalities of wealth were eliminated. There was the promise of economic growth and a higher standard of living. More social opportunities were opened up. To achieve these ends quickly, drastic measures were necessary. However, was implementing the Soviet model of the centralised command economy the best way to prosperity? Could efficiency and higher living standards have been achieved without authoritarian rule? Was the loss of political liberty worth the price? One ruling élite had replaced an older one, and the new élite was actually more ruthless, able to use modern methods of mass manipulation and control, especially the media, and was prepared to use force if necessary to stay in power. Large bureaucracies seemed to become more concerned with maintaining themselves in power than making progress towards some nobler political or social ideal.

Economic and social progress was achieved over 40 years, but at great personal and political cost. Some of the Eastern and Central European states were more forward-looking than the pre-war regimes they replaced, but none of them was as politically or economically mature as the more advanced states of Western Europe. They did sustain high growth rates in the immediate postwar decades. In the 1950s Communist economies actually expanded at a faster rate than in the West, and people could believe in a forthcoming Socialist utopia. Countries like Romania and Bulgaria, beginning from a low industrial base, could achieve rapid growth rates in a relatively short time, particularly since authoritarian regimes could forcibly hold down consumption in favour of investment. Even more sophisticated economies like Czechoslovakia and East Germany achieved promising results at first.

However, growth rates declined in the 1970s and 1980s. Partly this was due to external factors such as the world oil crisis of the early 1970s. Partly the fault lay in the planned economies themselves. The Stalinist central command economy model was fundamentally inefficient, paid little attention to quality, and was in essence a crude mechanism for ensuring growth in certain key areas at the expense of others. Resources were allocated and used wastefully, and the lack of technological innovation compared to Western Europe was a major handicap. Some private or cooperative ownership was encouraged in most Eastern Bloc countries, apart from Poland, where most land was privately owned and managed. However, in these countries the state was responsible for over 90 per cent of National Income and industrial output until the late 1980s. Ironically, the small private sector was remarkably more efficient.

COMECON failed to boost trade performance significantly. More enlightened economists and politicians tinkered with the system - Hungary was a prime example - but tinkering could not make Eastern European economies capable of competing with the West. Communist economic reformers who tried to introduce elements of a market economy into a socialist structure, for example by making consumer demand a criterion for determining production, still had to confront the reality of the central plan. It was the plan which determined overall priorities, and the state which determined overall investment and pricing policies, and often controlled foreign trade. Ideological and bureaucratic obstructionism also diminished the effectiveness of efforts to develop 'socialist mixed economies'. These did not work effectively in the long term.

2 Why, once opposition snowballed in the late 1980s, were the Eastern Bloc Communist regimes overthrown in a relatively short time?

> **KEY ISSUE** What common factors were there in the experiences of the collapse of the Communist regimes?

Taking a longer-term perspective, the Eastern Bloc regimes collapsed because they failed to deliver what the populations had been promised: a sustained rise in living standards and guaranteed employment. Also, by the 1980s, it was clear that the USSR would not use the Brezhnev Doctrine to crush radical change: therefore native Communist regimes could no longer command support on the grounds that their rule was preferable to a Soviet invasion and occupation. The threat of Soviet intervention was increasingly hollow after Gorbachev made it clear that he would not support reactionary regimes.

By the 1980s many Communists accepted that radical economic reform was necessary. It was difficult to implement without accompanying political reform and a change in attitudes. However, such a challenge to the accepted orthodoxy was unacceptable to many Communists. Reformers who in the past had gone beyond the bounds, as in Czechoslovakia in 1968, had paid the penalty. What changed was that Soviet leader Gorbachev recognised in 1985 the need for a more open society and political liberalism in the USSR if the initiative, individuality and adaptability necessary for economic reform were to flourish. He was no longer prepared to back established Eastern Bloc regimes which were reluctant to reform themselves. This was crucial, for example, for the course of events in East Germany. Without Soviet backing or the advantages of sustained economic progress, it was difficult for the regimes to resist growing popular pressure from populations aware that life was better elsewhere.

Once popular pressure forced change, as in Poland, the impetus snowballed elsewhere – the 'domino effect' – especially as it became clear that the USSR would not directly intervene. Even an isolated state like Romania was eventually affected. Reformers within the Communist ranks tried to adapt and save their parties. In Poland and Hungary, Communists realised early on the need for popular support to legitimise their continuation in power, and they tried to persuade opposition groups to join them and carry out economic reforms. The East German and Czechoslovak Communists were slower to adapt. All attempts were at best only partially successful. Although, apart from Romania, the transition to a new order was relatively free of major violence, once the Communists had entered into negotiations with other parties they found that their own credibility and institutional base were undermined. Ironically, in countries where Communists did try to reform the system from within, like Poland and Hungary, they did poorly in the subsequent free elections. However, in those countries where the Communists did far less to promote change - Bulgaria, the GDR and Czechoslovakia - they did better at the polls! But could any Communist regime based on one-party rule and Marxist orthodoxy survive and compete in a pluralistic society? Even in Bulgaria, where the weakness of the opposition enabled the Communists to put up a good showing, the opposition parties began to improve their standing after the elections, despite their continuing tendency to fragment easily. It seemed doubtful whether former Communists would be able to regain credibility in the long term.

3 What were the prospects for the post-Communist regimes?

> **KEY ISSUE** What problems and opportunities confronted the post-Communist regimes of Central and Eastern Europe?

At the time of writing this was the most difficult question to answer. Communist regimes in the Eastern Bloc were dismantled with varying speeds. In Romania and Bulgaria, for example, old traditions died hard and a considerable amount of Communist influence survived after 1989. Communists still existed, even if the names of their parties changed, and several remained influential in public life.

After 1989, or even before, old political parties were revived or new ones formed. Their prospects were not always promising. Most lacked traditions, organisation, popular leaders, money, mass membership or clear policies. They frequently divided into factions and lacked the discipline and relative unity of the old Communist parties. Whilst most parties agreed on the need to dismantle state socialism, there were disagreements about the pace of change. Some parties had nationalist aims. Nationalist parties, which sometimes represented particular ethnic minority groups (for example the Turks in Bulgaria), could exert considerable influence in new parliamentary systems where coalitions governed and it was difficult to command majorities. Some parties appealed more to rural than urban constituencies. Agrarian parties were still important in Poland, but less important in other countries than before 1939, because of the inroads of industrialisation and urbanisation. More right-wing parties like the Civic Democrats in the Czech Republic often had most attraction for professional middle-class citizens.

All the parties operated in societies without democratic traditions, or at least recent ones. Popular euphoria evaporated soon after 1989 as people realised that the overthrow of Communism did not mean utopia. The turnout at parliamentary elections fell as the novelty of free and open polling wore off. Opinion polls gave the clear message that ordinary people were dissatisfied with the development of democracy and the pace of reform, and felt that things had been better under Communism.

Difficult political decisions had to be made. The new democracies had to try to strike a balance between strong and effective leadership, usually in the form of a presidency, and a parliament with enough power to ensure the accountability of governments. This had not been experienced in the previous 40 years. Possibly because there had been a tradition of strong presidents in prewar Central Europe, for example Pilsudski in Poland, the preference was usually for strong parliamentary systems. However, a multiplicity of parties sometimes prevented strong and stable government. Elected presidents usually lacked presidential parties to give them effective power. In Hungary and Bulgaria the presidential office was largely ceremonial; in Poland presidential power was strengthened at the expense of parliament.

Political and economic prospects were often linked. New regimes inherited economic difficulties not of their making, but they were expected to resolve them, and indeed had to in order to maintain their credibility. Yet the transition from state-run to market economies, which most reformers expected, was fraught with difficulties. There were no precedents for such a transition. The economies not only lacked the traditions of private entrepreneurial initiative but also lacked institutions like commercial banks and stock markets which oiled the wheels of established capitalist economies. Also democratic governments were less able than their Stalinist predecessors to hold down workers' expectations and enforce labour discipline.

Should economic reform proceed rapidly or cautiously? There were doubts whether expectant populations would accept the sacrifices imposed by austerity programmes. It was difficult for governments to proceed with deregulation and denationalisation on a fair and rational basis. How would new economies compete with each other and with the West, and would the vices of capitalism be imported along with the good things? Inefficient enterprises and their workforces would suffer when supply and demand determined output. New governments found it difficult to cope with unemployment and the demands on social services. The East German example, after unification with prosperous West Germany, was not a promising one, since the East Germans suffered from problems such as unemployment and a rising cost of living.

Whilst enterprising individuals did well out of the changes and became the new privileged élite, living standards for the majority of working people in the former Eastern Bloc states dropped by up to a third within two or three years of 1989. The removal of subsidies on goods, services and housing, the loss of child-care benefit for women, the ending of many benefits once provided by enterprises themselves, made conditions worse even for those in employment. In Poland the health service budget declined by 42 per cent in 1991 alone. By 1992 unemployment was as high as eight per cent in Czechoslovakia and Hungary, and 14 per cent in Poland and Bulgaria (the real figures were probably much higher), percentages unknown in Communist days.

The dismantling of authoritarian rule brought other problems. Nationalist tensions were released. Czechoslovakia split into two, albeit peacefully. But other countries with national minorities experienced difficulties within their own borders. There were ethnic Hungarians in Romania and Turks in Bulgaria. National minorities were sometimes made scapegoats for other ills. Could national aspirations be satisfied without major upheavals?

Some of the new regimes, although nominally democratic, passed repressive laws. This happened in Slovakia and Poland, where the church again became linked to the state. Women in Eastern and Central Europe generally achieved little from the changes of regime. In some states new laws were passed against abortion, and women remained second-class citizens. In post-Communist societies there was actually a decline in the number of women in politics and especially senior government posts. Women featured prominently in the growing unemployment statistics.

On the international level, there was also the question of security and the place of Eastern and Central Europe in the post-Cold War world. The states in question, traditionally sandwiched between Russia and Germany, saw many attractions in a new 'Central European bloc.' The Czech President Václav Havel told the Polish Parliament in January 1990 that

1   We have a real historic chance to fill with something meaningful the
    great political vacuum that appeared in Central Europe after the
    breakup of the Hapsburg Empire. We have the chance to transform
    Central Europe from a phenomenon that has so far been historical and
5   spiritual into a political phenomenon ... Paradise on earth has not
    been victorious and there are many difficult moments ahead. All we
    have is the hope that we will return to Europe as free, independent and
    democratic states and nations ... Western Europe is substantially
    further forward in the process of integration. If we decide to return to
10 Europe individually, it will be substantially more complicated than if we
    enter into a mutual agreement ... We want a comity of European
    nations: independent and democratic states; a Europe which is stable,
    not divided into blocs and pacts; a Europe that does not need the
    protection of the superpowers.

For the new regimes, the attractions of the European Union were considerable, but it was obvious that it would be many years before their political and economic systems would be developed enough to make full membership realistic.

The issues outlined above were not academic but vital questions that needed to be resolved if the ending of Communist rule were to prove ultimately beneficial. Failure to come to terms particularly with economic problems and adjustment to the post-Communist world raised the fear that progress towards democracy would be discredited. Would Communism, feeding off the nostalgia for a more secure past, prove attractive again? There was a danger that new authoritarian regimes of the Left or the Right might arise. The gains of earlier years might be undone, and the hopes so evident on the day that the Berlin Wall was breached might prove hollow. The best hope for the former Communist states might be that they be integrated into other institutions like the European Union, so that Western liberal and democratic traditions would be grafted on to the developing democracies of Eastern and Central Europe. Or could they go their own way and still prosper?

Answering structured questions and essay questions on 'Conclusion'

In addition to questions on specific events, for example the Czechoslovakian crisis of 1968, and on specific countries, you are likely to encounter more general questions about Eastern and Central Europe in the second half of the twentieth century. Sometimes the questions will span the whole of the period covered by this book. Sometimes they will focus on a narrower period, for example that of approximately five years from the end of the Second World War, during which time Communist regimes consolidated their power. Occasionally particular countries will be mentioned in the essay title, sometimes not. In the latter case you may use the examples of individual countries to illustrate particular points. Whilst it is not necessary to always refer in detail to all the countries described and analysed in this book, you will require a reasonably wide-ranging knowledge to tackle such general questions effectively. Knowledge of one or two countries is unlikely to be enough.

The following are examples of more 'general' questions:

1. Account for the rapid establishment of Communist control in Eastern and Central Europe in the aftermath of the Second World War.
2. With reference to any *two* of the following states, explain why Communist regimes succeeded in retaining power for so long after 1949: the GDR (East Germany); Poland; Czechoslovakia; Hungary; Bulgaria; Romania.
3. Compare and contrast the process by which Communist power was established *or* overthrown in any *two* states of Eastern and Central Europe between 1945 and 1991.

The key words and phrases in essay 1 are 'Account for' and 'rapid establishment of Communist control'. The main theme is clear: Communist control was established in all the states of the region in the years between 1945 and 1949. Whilst it is not necessary to analyse events in all the Eastern Bloc states in detail, you should if possible refer to all the six countries dealt with in this book, and possibly focus on at least three in reasonable detail. The key point in this essay should be not just to *describe* the process of the Communist takeover country by country, but to *analyse* the reasons for the takeover, and where possible to make a genuine comparison and contrast between the experiences of different countries where appropriate. It is possible to do this in an introduction and a conclusion, but it is better done in the main body of the text.

To tackle this particular essay meaningfully, it is necessary to establish a context for your argument. This requires, as in this book, not just an account but also an analysis of what happened in the relevant countries during the Second World War. In particular you should examine the role of the Communists. It was not just native Communist activity and the exertion of Soviet influence, direct or indirect, which played a crucial role in extending Communist power. You must also consider other factors, such as the degree of popular support enjoyed by the Communists (which varied from country to country); the power vacuum which existed in these countries in 1945; the lack of democratic traditions; the part played by the Communists' rivals. If possible analyse which of these factors carried most weight in particular countries, and at particular times, and consider whether any general themes emerge.

The key words in essay 2 are 'reference to any two', 'explain why' and 'succeeded in retaining power for so long'. The theme is clear: although Communist regimes were overturned at the end of the 1980s, they had all managed to remain in power for several decades. Why was this? The question is not asking for an analysis of *why* and *how* the Communist regimes came to power, although that may be partially relevant to the question (for example, the methods employed by the Communists to defeat their opponents, and the use of Soviet influence, were in evidence after 1949 as well as before). There are several factors to be considered: the role of the USSR; the tactics of propaganda, manipulation and intimidation employed by one-party authoritarian regimes; economic progress, at least initially. When Communist regimes were seriously threatened, or Communist reformers themselves proposed radical policies, there was the threat of outside intervention, as became a reality in Hungary and Czechoslovakia. To what extent did the regimes have any popular backing, and to what extent were they dictatorial regimes, sustained ultimately by force? The important point as ever, is that you should *argue* a case, with appropriate analysis and supporting evidence.

The key words and phrases in essay 3 are 'compare and contrast', 'established **or** overthrown', 'any **two** states' and 'between 1945 and 1991'. You have considerable flexibility with this question, given that you can select specific countries and you can choose to consider either the establishment of Communist power or its demise. The important point is that you make a genuine *comparison and contrast*, throughout the answer, and not simply recount what happened. Analyse *why* the processes occurred as much as *how* they occurred.

Further Reading

There are many books dealing both with the general history of the region covered by this book, and also with individual countries which made up the former Communist states of Central and Eastern Europe. However, relatively few of them deal specifically with the period after 1945, relatively few cover the period beyond the late 1980s, and very few are written for students at the age and level at which this book is aimed. However, it is important, especially if you are studying for examinations in modern European history or European studies, that you do read at least a few good books or sections of them. The following titles are those which should help you understand more about the topics covered in this book. Since books on individual countries tend to be very specialised, these suggestions are books which cover the whole region or a major part of it.

R. Crampton, *Eastern Europe in the Twentieth Century* (Routledge, 1994). A useful general history of the region.

ed. J. Held, *The Columbia History of Eastern Europe in the Twentieth Century* (Columbia University Press, 1992). This comprises a history of each country in the Eastern Bloc from the early twentieth century to about 1990, and is useful in particular for establishing the background and the general context of events.

G. Swain and N. Swain, *Eastern Europe Since 1945* (Macmillan, 1993). This is a lucid history of the Eastern Bloc between 1945 and the early 1990s. It deals with all the countries of the Eastern Bloc, and is useful for drawing out some of the general themes.

P. Lewis, *Central Europe Since 1945* (Longman, 1994). This useful text covers the period from the Communist takeover to the post-Communist regimes of the early 1990s. It does not take a country-by-country approach, but is good at considering the context of events and analysing regional themes such as economic development.

J. Batt, *East Central Europe From Reform To Transformation* (Pinter Publishers, 1991). This title is strong on the political and economic implications of the transition from Communist to post-Communist rule.

D. Mason, *Revolution in East-Central Europe* (Westview Press, 1992). This provides a useful general survey of the period from 1945 to the early 1990s, then deals in more detail with the dramatic events of 1989 to 1992.

ed. S. White, J. Batt and P. Lewis, *Developments in East European Politics* (Macmillan, 1993). This is quite a specialised study, covering the late 1980s and the early 1990s, but for students wanting detail on political developments in specific Eastern Bloc countries at the time of the 1989 revolutions and their immediate aftermath it contains useful detail.

T. Ash, *We The People - The Revolution of 1990* (Penguin, 1990). A vivid journalist's account of events in Poland, Czechoslovakia and Hungary as Communist rule collapsed.

K. Crawford, *East Central European Politics Today* (Manchester University Press 1996). A detailed and useful comparative study of how the states of the former Eastern Bloc developed in the first decade after the collapse of the Communist regimes.

R. Pearson, *The Rise and Fall of the Soviet Empire* (Macmillan Press 1998). A useful survey of the period between 1945 and the early 1990s, covering key events and issues in Eastern and Central Europe, and particularly useful on relations between the various regimes and the USSR.

Index